ELEVATE YOUR CAREER

MORE IMPACT + MORE INCOME

Erin Urban

©2020

E. Urban Book Praise

"If you want a future filled with more successful habits than you imagined possible, then you need Erin Urban's Elevate Your Career. You will find a powerful roadmap that is enjoyable to read, easy to understand and simple to apply. Based on many of Erin's inspiring personal experiences and insights from clients' successes, Elevate Your Career contains much wisdom and many practical steps you can immediately implement that will significantly increase your leadership, influence, impact and income. If you only read one book this year - make it this one!"

- Rob Pennington, Ph.D., Educational Psychologist and Award-winning Author, DrRobSpeaks.Com

"If you're stuck in career quicksand, despite the fact that you're "driven" and "work hard", then grab this book today. It's an invaluable roadmap to elevating your career by being intentional about your behaviors, daily habits, relationships, and perception management. Thanks, Erin, for writing this book!"

- Curt D. Mercadante, Branding Expert and Bestselling Author, *"Five Pillars of the Freedom Lifestyle"*

"This book is a must-read for anyone entering, progressing or transitioning in their careers. Packed with practical tips and guidance from well researched work by someone who has gained first-hand experience of learning and growth through some hard knocks. Each chapter, each page, contains rich insights and immediate takeaways which is not easy to come by from today's bookshelves. Erin Urban has a gift of writing in language, making it easy and a joy to turn over the pages in this book. In addition to individuals, the content in this book would serve as a great aid-memoir for teams and HR organizations."

- Evelyn MacLean Quick, Former CPO, HESS Corp.

"Your pathway to success starts the minute you remove the roadblocks and mental barriers that have been preventing you from achieving career fulfillment. In "Elevate Your Career" Erin brings to life that career fulfillment starts with us. It begins with freeing your mind and uncovering who you are and were meant to be. The impact you have on others starts with the impact you have on yourself. "Elevate Your Career" will lead you to elevating your spirit and self-worth."

- Larry Levine, International Best-Selling Author of *"Selling From the Heart"* and Co-Host of the Selling From the Heart Podcast

"Erin Urban has written a must-read primer for anyone looking to Elevate their Career. She combines life experiences with practical advice. Read this book and learn from one of the best"

- David P. Tusa, President & Chief Executive Officer

"Yellow-Highlighter Worthy! Reading Erin Urban's "Elevate Your Career, More Impact + More Income", I found myself spending too much time highlighting brilliant passages rather than reading for review. Using her real-world client work to illustrate so many good personal management practices, I applaud Erin, her work, and her writing—especially as she offers herself up as "client #1". There is nothing she writes that she hasn't done for herself. I offer up for your consideration only one of my highlighted favorites: "The power of reflection is vastly underrated and often overlooked." Find your highlighter before you begin your read of Erin Urban's book."

- Rick Gillis, Speaker & Author, *"Leveling the Paying Field, a Groundbreaking Approach to Achieving Fair Pay"*

Legal Disclaimer

ISBN: **978-0-578-82082-8**

Connect with Erin Urban

www.coacheurban.com

www.linkedin.com/in/erinurban

www.elevateyourcareerbook.com

Dedication

I dedicate this book to my Mom.

It's because of the solid foundation that you provided, Mom, that I have the courage, tenacity, and fierce passion to empower people's lives for the better.

Acknowledgements

This book would not be possible if it were not for the unshakable faith in my potential and timely mentoring of David Wells. Your support and embodiment of what leadership truly is helped me transform my career and my life. Thank you for being the catalyst to fuel my ability to elevate my career and go on to achieve my wildest dreams.

All the great coaches will say that they always learn from their clients. This is certainly the case for me as well. Steven Fein, you have my heartfelt 'Thank You' for challenging me to write a book and reach those who may need to hear my message so they can elevate their careers.

And, to my husband, for being there regardless of how stressed I occasionally became during the growth spurts of my business (and writing a book). Thank you for helping me balance my naturally over-achieving nature with your calm, centered outlook.

My clients are the reason I have such a passion sharing how straightforward transformational change can be. I love being a part of your journey and seeing you unlock your potential!

Table of Contents

Author's Preface

Are you a driven, experienced professional that isn't seeing the career results you want and you don't really know why? Have you done all the right things (worked hard, taken on tough tasks, learned new skills, and tried to do your very best), but nothing is really moving the needle? You may feel like you've hit career quicksand and you aren't sure how to get unstuck. You've probably considered changing jobs, and maybe you already have, but it seems like you only traded locations with little impact.

Getting results in your career and seeing the growth you want should be simple to do. As a Certified Career Strategist and Executive Coach, it's my mission to close the gap between where you are today and where you want to be. I experienced a major career pivot that literally changed my life for the better. I want to share my journey, what I learned and now successfully apply with my clients to blow the lid off their potential.

This is the catalyst for this book: elevating your career for more impact and income is not mysterious, yet so few people seem to be able to connect the dots (myself included, many years ago). Career growth is straightforward. In fact, much of what influences positive change in your life is actually simple to achieve. The problem is, the process that genuinely works to improve your career gets buried by ancient career growth myths that keep us stuck and, often, frustrated.

You will be amazed at how specific, small, yet significant changes can drive powerful career uplifts. What keeps you unfulfilled at work has less to do with how great you are at your job and more to do with things that you may not have even considered. I am willing to bet that the reason you feel frustrated at the lack of results in your career is *not* due to any of the following reasons:

- Education and training
- Certification(s)
- Who you know
- How *much* you know
- Your experience level
- How long you've been at your company

You went to school and probably got decent grades. You chose a profession and you studied. You may have even gotten some experience at work before you "officially" started your career. On the job, you work hard and maybe put in extra hours. You try to be the very *best* at what you do. More than likely, you have the right credentials and/or plenty of experience. You might even think to yourself that your experience, work ethic, and results should speak for themselves.

The problem is that you still aren't seeing results and you don't understand why. After all, you did everything you needed to do to move up! You checked all the boxes—now what?

The major disconnect between what we *think* gets results is because of our belief in outdated career growth assumptions versus what actually works. We put entirely too much emphasis on hard skills. The key ingredient to turn your skills into real growth is often practically ignored.

What I'm talking about is your interpersonal skills and presence, or you how you "show up" around other people. This is often (pathetically) referred to as "soft skills." There's nothing soft about them. They are real and if you do not develop them, the gap between where you are now and where you want to go can be so big that if you slip, you will land right on your face. Ignoring so-called soft skills has hard consequences.

Interestingly, achieving real career results is heavily weighted to those more adept in interpersonal skills. Most of us know someone who has moved up in their career and has no idea what the heck they are doing, but they are likeable! Your ability to influence others allow you to achieve much more in life than credentials or hard skills alone will ever produce.

The reason soft skills are often overlooked in favor of hard skills is that they sound, well, *soft*. Soft skills seem squishy, intangible, fluffy, and, therefore, easily ignored. I felt the same way for a good portion of my life until my career transformation point, which changed everything. After my career wake-up call, I realized that soft skills are the gateway to developing interpersonal skills and influence.

The real truth is that your career success is a direct result of your expertise and your interpersonal skills, not one or the other. You need both.

Interpersonal skills are the *catalyst* to leverage your hard skills. They are also, unfortunately, mystifying, confusing, or intimidating to many people. Your interpersonal abilities are a multidimensional matrix of your mindset, behaviors, people skills, presence, and communication abilities (often referred to as "emotional intelligence" or EI). Everything from your attitude, what you say, how you say it, to your body language is involved.

Let's put it this way: you *drive* your credibility, but you do not *determine* it—other people do. This can be a hard concept to accept. As a result, many well-meaning professionals ignore the importance of honing their interpersonal abilities and managing perceptions!

To make matters even more seemingly complex and daunting to most people: your mindset is the major player in this game. Every single client that I have worked with has had a career roadblock rooted in their mindset, which shows its ugly self in their behavior somewhere (and often when they do not realize or want it).

The purpose of this book is to share with you a process by which to develop the intentional professional *presence* you want while increasing your impact and, as a result, your income.

The process to successfully shift your behavior and better manage others perceptions is actually quite straightforward although making the change isn't always easy. The key is knowing where to *start*. Most importantly, I know how powerful this process can be. I've experienced the results of focused career growth firsthand in my own life and have seen it repeated hundreds of times in my clients.

Even better: it does not take long to achieve the career results you desire. I successfully achieved a major career uplift in nine months and I know you can too! Most of us have habitual behaviors and some of them even sabotage our careers, just as I was doing as a young professional (more on that later).

The process to elevate your career is not about becoming someone you *are not*; it's actually about freeing your mind from career myths that keep hundreds of thousands of professionals stuck. It's about going from frustrated to fulfilled by creating a career action plan to open the door to more opportunities. **It's time to become the best version of yourself!**

Erin Urban

Chapter 1: Introduction

*"And how ironic that the difficult times we fear might ruin us
are the very ones that can break us open and help us blossom into
who we were meant to be."*
- Elizabeth Lesser

The Day That Changed Everything

The best thing that happened to my professional career was receiving *negative* feedback on my 360° peer review. Before you start thinking that either I'm a saint or crazy, let's be clear on the fact that I did not have an "aha" moment right away. That would be asking a lot from someone who, up until that fateful day, had very little self-awareness and a snarky attitude. I was like many people: convinced that my hard work would "speak for itself" and I did not consider myself influential. Even worse, I had no concept of the impact of my attitude on my career.

I remember the day of my pivot point distinctly. I had expected the standard performance review dialogue, which would—again—result in the usual pat on the back and no real career growth or paycheck increase. Instead, about halfway through the process, I heard: "You have performed well this year as usual; however, *we have some concerns.*"

The last four words are not what you want to hear in your performance review. While I was recovering from my surprise the HR manager went on to explain that I had received less-than-stellar marks on my 360° peer review. Apparently, even though I was technically adept, acknowledged as a hard worker, applauded for successfully managing difficult clients, and exceeded expectations on deliverables, I was not as robust at building relationships *inside* the company.

More specifically, my communication style tended to be abrupt, excessively blunt, and occasionally abrasive. To more sensitive souls, I was unapproachable and too focused on results. There was a general feeling that I didn't really care about the people I worked with beyond their positions. The well-meaning advice from the HR manager was for me to take my coffee cup around in the morning to "get to know people."

My first thought upon hearing this was: "Really, so I have to win a popularity contest now?" Before you laugh too hard or moan in despair, wait, it gets better!

While I would like to say that I immediately saw the error of my ways and had a transformation in my attitude *at that moment*, that's not how it worked. My response was unfortunately on par with my mindset at the time. "Do you want me to get my work done or chit-chat with people?" I asked. I was absolutely furious! My anger was so intense, I'm surprised that I didn't levitate from the room.

You see, like many hard-working professionals, I had a belief system that you didn't come to work to make friends. This same belief demanded that I be metrics and solutions-driven, held accountable for my outcomes, and measured by my wins. In other words, there wasn't much (if any) room for "personal stuff" at work. To me, there should be a clear line between work and personal. Those who delivered results got rewarded...or so I thought.

For the rest of that day, and for several weeks afterwards, I felt unappreciated, incensed, misunderstood, and frustrated. I remember thinking: "I work hard, and *this* is the thanks I get? I stay late on Fridays when most people go home at 4:00 p.m. I come in on the weekends to make sure my projects go smoothly. I put 150% into all of my work and I try to be the very best at what I do. Couldn't management clearly see that I was too busy to get involved with idle gossip? I have to get work done!"

The Breakthrough

After a few weeks of intermittently feeling sorry for myself or furious, the CEO of the company stopped me in the hallway at work one morning. He (and probably everyone else in our small company) was aware that I was unhappy with the outcome of my performance review. After a short chat, the CEO gave me a personal development book on effective communication. Because I greatly respected him, I took the book home and started to read it that very evening.

By the third chapter, my belief structure started to crumble. The very foundations of my professional persona were shaken. I remember thinking, "Why isn't this information taught in high school or college? I could have saved years of wasted time and frustration!" I had never actually read a self-improvement book before. I thought that self-improvement books were for people with problems. I certainly didn't think I had any *real* problems.

More importantly, I had no idea that I could actually change how I communicated or even control how I responded to situations, which would result in changes in my professional success. I was completely unaware that I could have that level of influence over *myself*. I was, until that moment, blind to my blind spots. I certainly had no clue how critical perception management was! **It dawned on me that my behavior at work could be sabotaging my career growth aspirations.**

Until that fateful performance review, I had been beating my head against a glass ceiling so hard that my head hurt. I didn't understand why I wasn't chosen for a management position when I was clearly excellent in my work, diligent, determined, and delivered results. I was a stellar project manager and known for handling more challenging accounts. I was frustrated that my results had not inspired any rewards from upper management.

The problem was that I was also rigidly professional at work. I was convinced that that was how you were *supposed* to behave. The wall between my work and personal life was so high you couldn't see over the top. I had little respect for those who took the time to chat at work. I am action-oriented and I equated soft skills with being soft-headed. I was a hard-driving overachiever and was laser-focused on results. In other words, I was a real pain in the butt to work with.

The Turning Point

Sometimes, we need a swift kick in the rear to get us motivated. The negative feedback on my 360° peer review was the catalyst I needed to elevate my career. Thanks to that experience and the revelations from the book recommended by the CEO, I was waking up. I started to realize that my habitual behavior might be working against me. I was also extremely excited to learn that I could change who I was for the better and that rocked my entire world!

Since it was obvious that my most glaring gap was my ability to build relationships—specifically, how I communicated (or didn't) with others—I went to work on applying my newfound knowledge. Based on my reading, I could shift how I communicated to better align my intent with the words I chose and my body language. Basically, I was becoming more intentional about how I "showed up" at work. Even though I only made small changes to start, the results were stunning.

Not only were people more responsive to a kinder, less forthright manner of communicating, they were also more friendly towards me. At first, I was concerned that my behavior change would reflect poorly in my project results. I thought (for some reason) that people wouldn't respect you if you were too nice and polite. It amazed me to discover that the opposite was true. Instead of people being less responsive to a more considerate and engaging me, they were *more* so. After a few weeks of interacting differently with my coworkers, some even provided information *before* I asked for it.

11

I was shocked. All this time I thought I had to be a hard driver to get respect and leverage a little intimidation when necessary. I honestly believed that when people were reluctant, you should lean harder on them. This is probably the reason that my nickname, which I found out much later, was the "Steamroller." What I learned was that people respond more positively to a caring attitude. **Those who take the time to get to know others beyond their positions and communicate more empathetically get better results.**

I also learned that:

1. It doesn't matter how much you know; it matters how well you connect with other people.
2. Your success is directly determined by your behavior, particularly towards other people.
3. All the education, expertise, and experience in the world will not overcome a lousy attitude.
4. No one likes working with an overachieving perfectionist because you make everything harder on everyone (especially yourself).
5. We are blind to our blind spots, but other people aren't.

Growing Into Influence

Hard on the heels of this experience, my mentor at work (who thankfully saw that I had potential) included me in his leadership development program that he normally reserved for managers. By this time, I realized that there was more to effective career growth than I had previously thought. I was already sold on the power of self-development, so when my mentor included me in his program, I was ready!

Our first assignment was to dive into a book called *The 5 Levels of Leadership* by John Maxwell. Since I was a newbie to this whole personal development thing, I'd never heard of one of the world's leading authorities on leadership. My first key takeaway from Maxwell's book was the revelation that **how leaders succeeded was the complete opposite of how I historically behaved at work.**

I'm ashamed to admit that I really didn't see the need to get to know people beyond their positions at work. I was taught to believe that you should be super professional in the workplace. Unfortunately, being super professional also made me super unapproachable. I was laser-focused on results, which didn't inspire trust from others. Why would you want to trust someone who obviously doesn't care who you are as a person as long as you deliver like a robot?

I also firmly believed, like many people, that more experience, knowledge, education, and credentials would automatically give you credibility (or a promotion). My belief structure falsely told me that people respected you because of your status, hard work, and what you achieved. However, as Peggy Klaus stated in her book, "75 percent of long-term job success depends on people skills, while only 25 percent on technical knowledge.",[1]

My world was being reshaped for the better. I finally recognized that having a people-first focus was a requirement for credibility and, ultimately, leadership. In reading Maxwell's books, and later becoming leadership development certified through his program, I learned the hardest lesson of all that saved my career: *we drive our credibility, but we do not determine it; other people do.*

Have you ever caught yourself thinking, "If I want something done right, I'll do it myself"? That was certainly my attitude. I did not understand why other people didn't do things just the way I would do them (like I had all the answers). I did not value other people enough. If there is one key lesson that I learned early in my career growth journey, it was how important other people are to your career success.

I didn't excel at collaboration; I thought this was something you did when you figured everything out and then needed to tell other people your decision. If there is one character trait that stands out for me, it is that I am determinedly independent. I am the product of an excellent upbringing by a single mom who instilled the value of being able to stand on my own two feet.

---

[1] Peggy Klaus, *The Hard Truth About Soft Skills: Workplace Lessons Smart People Wish They'd Learned Sooner.*(HarperCollins, 2007)

However, there's a fine line between being independent and not including anyone—even people who *should* be included.

During a one-on-one meeting with a manager very early in my career, years before my career wake-up call, she told me that she would "rather have a B- performer than an A+ employee who never communicated." I didn't understand it then, but now I see just how challenging I made her life as a manager. I solved problems by myself and didn't include anyone on my action items. I just got it done. I figured that's what you were supposed to do!

The gap I was innocently ignoring was the fact that my actions did not align with my intent. I had spent zero time and energy on my professional presence. I had also developed habits and behaviors that were undermining my outcomes. Additionally, I was completely unaware of other people's perception of my actions and, ultimately, how that was keeping me from achieving my goals.

The Leap into Leadership

This story has a happy ending. Less than a year after my pivot point performance review, I was offered a leadership position. It wasn't just *any* leadership role either; it required a person who excelled at developing relationships, motivating others, and building trust at a strategic level...and they picked *me*.

How does a person who was known as the "Steamroller" transform into a leadership role in nine months? It was superficially easy: I ripped the blindfold off, became self-aware, and did something about it. I went from me-focused to people-focused. It was like I had imprisoned myself in a cage made up of career myths and false beliefs for 30 years. I had to relearn what mattered most to drive the right perceptions, achieve success, and unlock my potential.

As I tell my clients, you do not have to make radical sweeping changes to get positive results in your life. You would be amazed at how impactful small, yet significant changes in behavior can truly be. The key is how sincere you are about those changes. For example, if I had read the books and applied the techniques without putting my heart into it, I would not have seen the same results. People can quickly sniff out inauthenticity.

After the 360° review, the revelations from my first self-improvement book and the knowledge I was applying from my mentor's leadership program inspired radical changes. For one, I personally felt better. I remember being distinctly annoyed about 65% of the time at work before my pivot point.

Historically, I let my emotions rule me instead of the other way around. Now that I was more aware, I was also more intentional about my thoughts, words, and actions. As a result, I was making *real* connections with people at work. Keep in mind that I had been working with these same people for more than three years. They had a pretty firm idea of who I was, but that perception was starting to shift for the better.

I changed how I responded, interacted, and communicated to a more thoughtful and collaborative manner. While many of the alterations in my behavior were subtle, it was telling how much of a difference they made. I paid more attention to my body language, tone of voice, and word choice. I also made the change internal. As Carl W. Buehner said, "They may forget what you said, but they will never forget how you made them feel." **I cared about how I made other people *feel* and it paid off.**

I was offered a leadership position within the same company where I had received negative feedback during my performance review less than a year previously. While most would consider their growth journey done after moving into a leadership role, I'm happy to say that mine had just begun. By that point, I realized that continual improvement is essential for a growth mindset. The moment you accept the status quo, you stagnate. You become irrelevant and you disconnect.

I had seen massive results from only a few small shifts in my behavior, which led to a tremendous increase in my influence (and my income). My next thought was, "What *else* can I accomplish?" I was curious and excited to see how much I could expand my career potential. When I accepted the leadership role, instead of saying, "I've arrived", I thought, "I've begun."

This experience ignited the spark that later inspired me to coach, speak, and train others to elevate their careers and increase their influence and impact. I focused on research, formal training, and achieved certifications to evolve into a career strategist and international speaker. I'm proud to say that I have helped thousands of driven professionals overcome their roadblocks to unlock their career (and life) potential. I look forward to sharing the journey with you!

Let's begin.

Chapter 2: Roadblocks to Growth: Career Myths

*"And that's the paradox of success: these beliefs that carried us here may be holding us back in our quest to go **there**."*
– Marshall Goldsmith

Career Growth Assumptions

If you are like I was, you might feel that having the experience, working hard, getting all the right certifications, and trying to be the best at your job is what it takes to get ahead. I wish that were true. It often gets you to a certain point in your career. However, without developing other skills, like emotional intelligence and agile communication, even the most experienced professional can get stuck.

On the flip side, those who have their interpersonal skills nailed don't get too far if they don't also have the expertise. **Your career success is a direct result of both your expertise *and* your interpersonal skills.**

I've identified seven main career myths that act as roadblocks to growth:

1. Focusing on IQ vs. EQ
2. Overachieving
3. Working hard
4. Overcommitting
5. Excessive independence
6. Super professionalism
7. Qualification dependence

In the case of my client Mary, she has all the expertise in the world and her team loves her. She excelled at working hard, overachieving, and (sometimes) overcommitting. Her peers and senior leaders though, noticed some gaps. Mary, like so many well-meaning and hard-working executive professionals, got where she is today through sheer grunt. "Grunt" is putting in the time, building your expertise, doing a great job, and doing what it takes to get results.

This attitude had gotten her pretty far…and pretty stuck. The 360° feedback that I conducted with 30 members of her team, peers, colleagues, and upper management came back as stellar in all but three categories: (1) she didn't behave like a leader; she acted like a manager, (2) she shared too many of her frustrations with almost everyone when she got wound up, and (3) she wasn't strategic enough and tended to take on too much.

Her senior leadership team liked the fact that she got results, but they didn't think she was the right type to move further up the corporate ladder. Worse, her team's morale suffered every time she vented. Mary has the expertise and she gets things done, which had gotten her to the role she was in, but in order to move up - she had to close the gap between where she was and where she wanted to go.

The skills she'd developed served her well to a point, but it was time to let go of the habits that no longer supported her growth. Even more pressing, she was up for a promotion; the pressure was on! Mary felt a little overwhelmed at first. Fortunately, all it took was just a few tweaks in her behavior for the changes to be recognized almost immediately.

Everyone's journey is different and most of us just need a few shifts to set our feet firmly on the path to more opportunities. While the phoenix rising image is attractively dramatic in our minds, a complete reinvention isn't necessary to get real results. What is most important right now is understanding what is standing in your way to elevate your career.

1. Focusing on IQ vs. EQ

As Zig Ziglar said: "No one cares how much you know, until they know how much you care." You can be brilliant, but if you behave like a jerk, you won't get the opportunities to leverage your brilliance. It's that simple. **Your IQ does not define success in your career or life.** Super smart professionals are highly respected and prized by their companies for their select skills. On the other hand, if their interpersonal skills need developing, it keeps them locked into limited positions or out of the managerial path.

If you feel like people just don't "get" you, or when you start talking about your area of expertise they find the first excuse to leave, then you probably have an EI (emotional intelligence) gap. As Daniel Goleman stated in his book, *Emotional Intelligence*: "Emotional aptitude is a meta-ability, determining how well we can use whatever other skills we have, including raw intellect."[2]

Your emotional intelligence is far more critical to your overall life success than your IQ. The problem starts in our public education system. We are rated, ranked, and graded based on our IQ, not our EI. We are conditioned to believe that good grades equal good results. At best, IQ contributes about 20% to the factors that determine life success, which leaves 80% to other forces.[3]

Other than having a case of the "smarts", most of us truly expect that we can leverage our education and expertise to get ahead in our careers. While these things are important, they are not always the deciding factor in whether you see the opportunities that you want. As I learned the hard way, being great at *what* you do doesn't mean that you are great to work with.

In the case of one of my clients, Stuart, being smart was actually getting in the way of the career opportunities he

---

[2] Daniel Goleman, *Emotional Intelligence* (Bantam Books, 2006), 36.

[3] Howard Gardner, "Cracking Open the IQ Box." *The American Prospect*, (Winter 1995).

wanted. He is a well-meaning, credentialed, and highly educated man. I say he "means well" because he had a tendency to share his knowledge with people whether they wanted it or not.

Stuart had absolutely no idea that his work colleagues and his boss found this slightly irritating. He was completely unaware that his smarts weren't always appreciated. His well-intentioned habit of adding unasked-for information to most conversations, automatically correcting others, and being critical of his colleagues' work was hurting his ability to build rapport with the people in his organization.

Likeability, which is an outgrowth of a higher EI function, determines how well you are able to rise in your career, connect with and influence others, build robust relationships, and, ultimately, generate more income. The most successful professionals are not necessarily the most educated or those with the highest IQ. What they *do* have in common is the ability to leverage their interpersonal skills to augment whatever expertise they have in order to fuel career growth.

2. Overachieving

Being the best at what you do does not make you a better person. It does not guarantee you a promotion, a pay raise, or even a pat on the back. In fact, it can do the opposite. **There's a difference between doing a great job and overachieving.** Overachieving, as strange as this may sound, is not always helpful for your career. It took me years to figure this one out.

We have been brainwashed to think that, by being the best, we are guaranteeing a great future. This is not always the case.

I will never forget when my client, Aria, called me about her new job. She had to leave a toxic workplace and was very excited to land a promising position. There were just a few hurdles. Right before her first day on the job, two of her peers quit. New management was looking to shake things up and create a more productive culture and these two individuals didn't want to participate, so they left. Aria informed me with pride that, even though she was working nights and weekends, she was managing both of their jobs and hers too!

When she asked me for my insight, I replied simply: "Aria, are they paying you three times as much and/or giving you a promotion for this extra work?" For a minute, there was silence on the other end of the line. She said slowly, "No, we haven't really talked about it. My boss is proud of me though." I then asked: "Does that mean your boss is going to pay you more?" By this time, she was catching on. "What should I do?" she asked. We discussed her options for opening a conversation about her current excessive workload and what the next steps need to be to either compensate her or get her additional support.

I'm not advocating for being lazy, marginal, or only just barely meeting expectations. There's nothing wrong with occasionally exceeding expectations, especially when strategically important. The problem with overachiever's syndrome is that you feel like you should *always* exceed expectations. There is a difference between a healthy level of ambition and excessive overachievement. If you are never really satisfied with your work, you may also suffer from perfectionism. If you are struggling with this concept, let me break it down for you.

Constantly overachieving can result in several things:

You could be so amazing in a particular role that you become invaluable. As a result, shifting roles or even getting a promotion can be difficult. Your management has come to rely on your skills and your tendency to over-deliver in your current role, and they don't want to lose that. In Aria's case, of course her boss was proud: he was getting three roles accomplished for the price of one!

If you strive to be the best, you could also intimidate others and incite jealousy or dislike. People do not like to be constantly reminded that they don't really measure up to your example. You may become the victim of workplace gossip and backstabbing. It is a very lonely place to be. I've been there and I do not recommend it.

You probably struggle to say "no." Because of this, you get dumped on and overwhelmed by all the extra work you take on. If you are also good at fixing things, you can become the firefighter that gets all the really nasty jobs no one else can or wants to handle. At first, you may feel awesome about this (your ego likes to tell you lies). After a while, though, it gets stressful and overwhelming.

People who excessively overachieve may suffer from burnout, isolation, anxiety, depression, and, very likely, health issues. You might end up leaving the company to find work elsewhere, only to repeat the cycle again and again. I commonly see these individuals suffering because work is constantly overriding their personal lives. If you have overachiever's syndrome, you may already notice the side effects in your health, at work, or at home.

Also, closely related to being a workaholic, overachievement usually has roots somewhere in your early career, who you looked up to as a child, or what was defined as important when you were a young adult. I encourage you to find the root cause to bring about a healthy balance in your work and in your life.

3. Working Hard

Doing more usually results in more of the same. What you want is more of something *different*. **Unfortunately, keeping your nose to the grindstone and working hard doesn't always result in the career growth you want.** Many professionals work really hard, hoping that someone will notice. When you think about it, this is a little silly.

In America, we have a "work hard, play hard" myth. Most people think their hard work speaks for itself. To me, this mindset is a hold-over from our pioneering, do-it-yourself culture. Two hundred years ago - you'd better work hard because, otherwise, you didn't eat. This isn't always the case in today's society. Very much like overachieving, "working harder" usually looks like:

1. Coming in early to the office because you feel that people who show up earlier are "better" workers. You may also scoff at those who have the nerve to leave early for family or other reasons.
2. Staying late at the office or showing up on weekends to demonstrate how dedicated you are to your job. There is a high likelihood that you also frequently talk about how hard you work.
3. Showing up at the office when you are sick, not feeling well, or injured. You might also confuse this with having "grit." In the case of being sick, all you have is *germs* and other people don't want them!

Get over it and stop flogging yourself. No one gets promoted because of good attendance anymore. If I see another "how to get up early and be a winner" book or article, I will gag. The hard work mindset is actually quite limiting. To some poor souls, they think just by working themselves to death it makes them a better person and guarantees some sort of reward. It does neither of these things.

You are better off being *efficient* at your job, not a harder worker. There is a huge difference between being busy and being productive. It's also highly likely that you are working so hard you miss opportunities to develop critical and strategic networks. Understand and meet the expectations for your role. If you are expected to simply put in longer hours, even if your role doesn't require it, find another place to work.

4. Overcommitting

I was a rampant overcommitter professionally and personally. I'm not sure why I thought I had more time in the day than other people. I constantly double and triple-booked myself, trying to squeeze so much in a day; it's surprising that I accomplished anything at all. As a result, I wasn't able to showcase my skills because one cannot do everything, be everywhere, or please everyone. Some people need to overcommit because they are afraid to upset anyone or say "no." Either way, it's self-defeating.

Sonia is a great example of rampant overcommitment. She wants to be in front of the decision-makers. It's important to her that she be a "known quantity", well-networked, a member (or on the board) of all the right organizations, and part of as many projects as possible at work.

One day, those decision-makers chose another colleague instead of Sonia for a promotion that she was *sure* she would receive. She was devastated. It was heartbreaking to realize that all of her involvement didn't mean anything. When we first sat down together, she shared that she felt unappreciated and was mystified about why she wasn't chosen for the role.

As a friend and long-time colleague, I could have told her why she wasn't chosen, but I wisely kept my mouth shut. Instead, I asked questions to hopefully start peeling back the blindfold her mindset had placed over her eyes. Sonia was known for several things because of her overcommitment—and it wasn't about being visible. Rather, she was known for:

- Always being late; I mean, *really* late. She was over 30 minutes late to our meeting!
- Sometimes forgetting meetings altogether and not showing up, then acting nonchalant about it.
- Rarely being 100% present, no matter where she was. Even her sister commented over dinner with family one night: "Sis, you're here, but you're *not* here. At least, not mentally."
- Struggling to follow up on action items and assignments, and often rushing the job, if not dropping the ball altogether.

It's not that Sonia was incapable. She has all the education and expertise she needs to succeed. She has great interpersonal skills and people genuinely like her. Unfortunately, she also thought that committing to a lot of things to get visibility equaled career growth. It doesn't. In fact, it can sabotage you. You are only allotted so many hours in a day or a week. If you commit to more than you can reasonably do in that amount of time, everything suffers.

Remember, when you say "yes" to one thing, you are also saying "no" to something else.

Unfortunately for Sonia, the executives at her company weren't seeing the smart, capable, and effective professional that she truly is. Instead, they saw someone who couldn't complete tasks, follow up, be effective, prioritize wisely, respect others' time, or even do the job she was given. Of course they didn't promote her. The good news is that there will be other opportunities. Regardless, it's a harsh lesson to learn the hard way!

If this is something you identify with, consider what areas at work you can extract yourself from. What is strategically significant and what can you let go of? Keep in mind that overcommitting *yourself* is different than being overcommitted. Thanks to our "work hard" culture and lean resources, many misguided bosses think that overcommitting their team is a guarantee to get more work done. In fact, it usually does the opposite and increases the attrition rate.

5. Excessive Independence

Figuring things out on your own is great, but no one develops inside of a vacuum. **Your career success is only as good as your ability to collaborate with others.** Independence doesn't mean it's a great idea to tackle everything on your own to prove how awesome you are. You are more likely to alienate yourself and stress out your manager.

What I see, particularly in emerging professionals, is a mindset that being independent is required to do your job well. Some professionals feel that they have something to prove by figuring things out without help. They can demonstrate how smart and capable they are by solving problems all by themselves. If this is your attitude, all you are demonstrating is that you are a poor collaborator. Involve and evolve!

Independent thought and decision-making skills are excellent examples of high emotional intelligence (known interchangeably as EI or EQ). Not involving others in your problem-solving journey because you (1) are afraid of looking stupid, (2) are unaware that others have good ideas too, or (3) have to prove a point are three traits found on the lower end of EI. On the other hand, collaboration with others is an excellent skill to develop.

As a bonus, when you collaborate with others, even when you don't feel you need to, you are more likely to gain their trust. Don't be afraid to bounce ideas around, get advice, or ask for help from other people. They will feel like you appreciate their input and it is a great way to acknowledge your respect for their expertise. You also build bonds and develop relationships much faster.

Note, however, that there's a difference between being a needy person who struggles to get things done and asking for help because you appreciate other people's knowledge. Please do not get swallowed up by the self-defeating idea that asking for insights, advice, or help is being a "bother."

A common sub-trait of this is the tendency to keep things to yourself until you've figured out all the answers or become the expert. It's better to ask for help and authentically share where you are in your journey with others. No one really expects you to be an expert at everything, unless you lied on your resume to get the job.

Occasionally, I hear this from new clients: "I really don't feel comfortable sharing until I know everything there is and become a subject matter expert." While this is significantly related to perfectionism, it's also common in those who constantly overachieve. You are only hurting your career growth and keeping everyone else in the dark. To make matters worse, you could be solving the *wrong* problem or providing a solution that falls short of the mark simply because you couldn't collaborate.

I used to be terrible at this. By the time the problem was half-way explained to me, I had already solved it (or so I thought). I took great pride in not only being excessively fast in my problem-solving skills. On the other hand, my managers did not prefer my lone wolf, wild card style. They also didn't appreciate me solving a problem that wasn't thoroughly investigated yet — or solving for the wrong problem.

My idea of collaboration was to inform people of what I had decided to do. Instead of involving them (managers or otherwise), I would do everything myself, leaving everyone else in the dark. I thought I was being smart. I am smart, but it didn't come through very well by acting this way. It cost me bonuses and promotions until I finally got a clue.

6. Super Professionalism

Another character trait that sabotaged my career growth was being too professional. **Gone are the days when formality got you ahead.** You don't look smarter; you just come off as distant and lacking empathy. Or worse, people feel that you think less of them or look down on them. If you mistakenly remind people how insignificant they are, they will show you how isolated you can become. Be *real* with people without being an oversharing weirdo.

I had simply assumed that you didn't come to work to make friends. I didn't chit-chat and I didn't discuss my personal life with those I worked with. I labored under the misapprehension that this was what I was supposed to do! Little did I know that it just made me extremely unapproachable. No one knew who I truly was until I loosened up a little.

The challenge is knowing what to share and when. It's also important to understand what being "too formal" looks like. In highly competitive environments, it may be frightening to let your guard down. Know your company culture and what the expectations are. As a rule of thumb, don't share something that can hurt you later. It's okay to smile, laugh when appropriate, show appreciation for others (often), and share select personal stories.

The roadblock for many is that they feel a certain demeanor or mask is necessary in the workplace. It may also be difficult for super professional people to break down the wall between work and personal life. You might feel that it's inappropriate to share anything about your life at work. Perhaps you aren't sure what to say or you are afraid that saying the wrong things can be used against you later.

If you struggle here, start with showing a genuine interest in others and take time to get to know them personally. This may help you with sharing more about yourself. A top tip that helps those who are locked in a super-professional cage is developing the art of being kindly and genuinely curious about others. When you ask questions about other people in order to know them better, you:

- Show that you care about them
- Demonstrate that you are willing to listen
- Begin to develop a rapport with others

If you have trouble opening up, you may find it easier to share something about yourself when you discover commonalities in others. People find it easier to build relationships with those that they can relate to. This also reduces the fear of being judged. Some people lock away their personal life because they fear the judgement of others.

By leveraging casual conversations, you can learn more about others so you will know what is appropriate to share. You can also start to build those relationships that are vital to seeing the career growth you want. Make a point to get beyond what people do at work. One of the major pitfalls I had was seeing people as their positions. Understandably, those I worked with felt like I didn't care about who they were as a person.

Being super professional at work is an outdated assumption held over from more traditional times. As company cultures evolve, there is increasing talk about being authentic in the workplace. If you feel like you are putting forward a facade at work, try sharing a little bit about yourself and getting to know those you are closest to on a deeper level.

7. Qualification Dependence

"I've got enough experience and I have an MBA—I should be a director," said one of my new clients. This is a sentiment that I've heard repeated in some form for years. **Your experience is not a guarantee of career growth.** If you want to elevate your career, it's time you learned that experience isn't the best teacher—*evaluated* experience is. Your credentials aren't a guarantee of growth either. Your ability to rise and develop is also determined by how well you interact with others and how they perceive your behavior.

Historically, companies have had a bad habit of promoting people just because they had experience as an *individual* performer. Two things usually happen in these instances: the company loses a great individual performer and gains a bad manager. Occasionally, it all works out, but the case has been made that your experience or credentials do not equal a career uplift.

Many professionals feel that getting all the right certifications is a guaranteed ticket to better opportunities. As you might guess by now, this is not the case. There is more to your career growth than having a bunch of letters after your name. In fact, it can be a giant waste of time and money if you are ignoring your own internal self-development needs.

A very good example of this is a former industry colleague of mine. He's a great guy, but it still hasn't dawned on him that obtaining all of the possible industry certifications doesn't make him an ideal hire or even qualify him for opportunities. Forget the credentials; what about your credibility? How great are you at developing relationships with people? I mean *all* types of people, not just those exactly like you.

He makes great connections with some, but others can't stand him. That's because he lacks awareness and the ability to adapt and align his communication style. This gap hurts his chances of being accepted by a broader audience. Your certifications do not guarantee success; your interpersonal skills do. Having additional characters after your name does not automatically make you a great person to work with or for. You know what else? **You don't decide if you are credible or not—other people do.**

Overcoming Your Roadblocks To Growth

Self-awareness is a huge first step to overcoming your roadblocks to career growth. Those that are not self-aware might be reactionary, rather than *responsive* (reflective, intentional, and adaptive) in situations. Instead of being intentional about your thinking, behavior, and communication, it's done from habit.

One of the reasons is simply because most people aren't even cognizant that they have control over their mindset, actions, and communication! It took me 30 years before I realized that I had a choice and finite control over my behavior. **Self-awareness is essential for growth because you cannot improve upon something you don't fully understand.**

The other reason we have behaviors that go unchecked for years (for some, an entire lifetime) is because our brains develop habits to save energy. This makes a lot of sense when you think about it. Just imagine waking up every day only to learn everything all over again. That would never work!

As a result Mother Nature has given us this wonderfully complex brain which helps us out by developing automatic response mechanisms – or habits. Unfortunately, our mental shortcuts are rarely ever fact-checked which can result in behaviors that actually do not serve our needs or wants. Becoming self-aware is the first step towards freedom!

How do you become self-aware? If you are reading this book, you are probably well on your way. People who are totally blind to their failings, or even worse, defiantly so (commonly found with fixed mindsets), typically don't go out of their way to seek change. *You have.* That means you are on the right track.

You can change your character, behaviors, habits, and presence to align with who you want to be. You don't have to accept the status quo and wallow in career stagnation. You don't have to stumble forward blinded by career growth myths and mystified about how to get the results you want. So many people have no idea that they *can* change. You can transform and this book gives you the process!

Now that we know the seven common career myths that are roadblocks to growth, let's get started on unlocking your potential for more impact and income!

Erin Urban

Chapter 3: The Atmosphere To Fuel Growth

"The passion for stretching yourself and sticking to it, even (or especially) when it's not going well, is the hallmark of the growth mindset."
- Carol S. Dweck

Creating A Growth Atmosphere

When it comes to self-development and career growth, you can only pivot when you are mentally ready. Reading a book, listening to a podcast, or watching an insightful video doesn't automatically create a catalyst for change. Wouldn't it be nice if that were the case? I'd ship this book to everyone in the world! However, that's like lighting a match on the moon. Chances are, unless you have the right atmosphere, it won't burn.

Take my career shift for example. The combination of being frustrated with the lack of career results, the fateful performance review, and the help of my leader and mentor enabled me to see positive change. Without it, I may not have been able to unlock my potential. My client, Mary, was told that she "wasn't executive material" a few months before she invested in career growth coaching with me. Sometimes we need an incentive to change and develop the right atmosphere for growth. Unfortunately, often this is through negative feedback!

In this chapter, we will review what the "right atmosphere" looks like. We will discuss what internal atmosphere creates the best environment for attainable and sustainable change while staying true to our authentic selves. Although we aren't reinventing ourselves, it does take some work to unlearn negative patterning and let go of the bad habits that no longer serve us. Basically, we need to develop awareness around which mindset we are feeding. **The mindset, habits, and behaviors we feed are the ones that drive us.**

Because I love steps and processes, I've identified four key areas that you need to be aware of before real self-development can take root and grow. Much of the focus work is internal to start. If you skip creating the right internal atmosphere, you might get a few results, but you will find it difficult to sustain them. It's also highly likely that you will eventually self-sabotage.

Here's something else you should know: *you don't have to be perfect before you start applying changes to see results in your career.* There is no such thing as "perfect." I wasn't perfect when I achieved my first leadership role; I had only just begun to unlock my potential. What makes this process transformational is the power of knowing that you can learn, apply, adjust, and make the next big step to elevate your career all at the same time!

1. Growth Mindset

All the insights in the world won't matter if you do not have a growth mindset. The fact that you are reading this book means that you are already on the right path. A closed or fixed mindset isn't open to challenging the mental image of yourself and your belief system. Fixed mindsets typically scoff at any reference to self-development, think that you cannot change, and also seek to validate their standpoint rather than being open to new ideas. They are looking for justifications to keep the status quo and avoid doing the work to change. It's what I call being "defiantly ignorant." Conversely, a growth mindset embraces the following:

Abundance Thinking

In many ways, our society has trained us to have a scarcity mindset. A scarcity mindset is one that constantly seeks to conserve; it is worried about itself and whether it will have enough. Such persons don't give out praise much (if ever) or even say "thank you" very often. People with this mindset justify not giving because they weren't given anything *first*.

Those who express abundance thinking tend to give freely (without expectation of return) and actually receive more than those who withhold. Think of it this way: how likely are you to be friends with or help someone who is scarce with acknowledgement, appreciation, or knowledge? Consider this for a moment and I think you will see my point. **Good things come to those who give.**

Curiosity

The more candles I collect on my birthday cake, the more I realize I don't know. It's a wonderful feeling! Imagine how boring life would be if you knew everything; there would be little to look forward to. Ask questions and be open to new ideas, concepts, and thoughts. **Think of change as a gift you can give yourself.** Those who aren't open or curious are always looking to justify their position. They are also afraid of change.

If you look forward to learning new things, it means you have a curious mind. When I was a teenager and a twenty-something, I thought I should already know everything. Now I look back at those times and just laugh! There are so many critical pieces of advice I would give my younger self, the most important of which is: *shut up and ask better questions.*

The saddest expression of fixed-mindedness and lack of curiosity was a manager that I briefly reported to when I was a young professional. He had decided that he had learned everything he was going to learn at the age of forty-five. From that point on, he refused to embrace anything new. It was like watching the walking dead. Seeing him struggle and merely exist in this locked routine inspired me to vow to always learn, no matter what age I am. I have been faithful to that vow.

Reflection

The power of reflection is amazing. Counterintuitively, experience alone is not the best teacher. **Just because you experience something does not mean that you automatically learn from it.** Do you know someone that keeps repeating the same drama over and over again? Chances are that they haven't paused to reflect and learn from their experiences.

I am often reminded of the importance of reflection with this quote from Confucius: "By three methods we may learn wisdom: first, by reflection, which is noblest; second, by imitation, which is easiest; and third by experience which is bitterest." The habit of reflection is invaluable in your career growth journey. It is also essential for maintaining the optimal mindset for growth, which we will learn more about later in this chapter.

Think of reflection as building mindset muscle. If you are a sports fan, you might already know that muscle strength isn't developed by exercise, but rather afterwards during refueling and rest. The same applies to the power of reflection. Your mindset isn't developed and elevated in the moment of experience, but rather through times of reflection.

Forward Focused

The forward-focused person does not accept the status quo and certainly doesn't wallow in the past. **While your experiences can enrich and inform you, they do not define you.** Again, it's incredibly important to let go of that which does not serve you. Being present while focused on the future is an important step here.

Those that are curious about what's to come in the future are less likely to allow minor setbacks to hamstring them. They understand that change is necessary for growth. The catalyst for change is also likely to occur from challenges. They know the importance of failing forward and trying new things in order to unlock their potential. They aren't as inhibited by temporary upheavals. Forward-focused people can see the big picture and are invested in long-term gains.

Mental Agility

When you are mentally agile, you are more adaptable to situations. This is an area where I've struggled in the past. I absolutely hate being disappointed and I'm a rampant planner. It's not that planning itself is bad, it's what you do when things don't go to plan. How do you respond? Can you adjust?

A person's ability to adjust to their environment and remain optimistic is important. Not only is this indicative of emotional intelligence, but it's also necessary for resilience and overall growth. If you are stumped by every change in your life, it will be difficult to adapt, overcome, and grow.

While I have always been good at overcoming obstacles, I spent way too much time wallowing in disbelief and disappointment about the unexpected. Things do not always happen according to plan. It's essential for your growth to make the most out of your experiences. Becoming hyper-aware about what you can actually control in your life is also very helpful. **When you realize that the only thing you can really control in this lifetime is yourself, it's easier to remain objective during situational challenges.**

2. Self-Appreciation

I was tempted to leave this part out because it's so deeply internal and personal. However, as a coach and as a person who has transformed my life for the better, self-appreciation is essential to long-term fulfillment. It is important that I include this key ingredient to your growth atmosphere. Almost everyone I know struggles with truly appreciating themselves. Even those who say that they do, show obvious signs of self-distrust or self-loathing. A good example of this is someone I care for a great deal. Amanda will tell you that she thinks kindly of herself; I disagree.

Amanda is a friend who has completed multiple Ironman and long-distance endurance events across the world. If you aren't familiar with an Ironman, you must swim 2.4 miles, transition to complete a 112-mile bike ride, and finish with a full running marathon of 26.22 miles—all in one day. I think that's marginally insane, and I've done some pretty crazy things myself! As a competitive athlete, I have a deep respect for the training that goes into these types of endurance events.

Regardless of how grueling it is and how well Amanda places in each event, she's never happy with her performance. She pushes herself beyond reasonable training expectations. As a result, Amanda often self-sabotages her goals because she pushes herself too hard. As a recovering perfectionist and a behavioral scientist, I know all too well that what she is doing to herself physically and mentally is a direct outgrowth of self-dislike. If you actually liked yourself, you couldn't do that to yourself. It's that simple.

Most of us do not appreciate (or even like) who we are. We aren't always encouraged to accept ourselves in a loving way. It's likely that you are not your own best friend. You probably say things to yourself that you would *never* say to someone you cared about. What's crazy is that this type of negative internal abuse is considered completely acceptable!

Most cultures program us to put ourselves last and think of ourselves as unworthy or unimportant under the mask of being "humble." However, there's humility and then there's self-flagellation. What I see in most cases is the latter. I would argue that almost every mentally "normal" person in the world has negative self-beliefs and false labels that erupt into issues that cause self-sabotage.

This becomes extremely poignant when you are working on self-development and career growth. Even in your professional life, how much you respect yourself is vital. Let's put it this way: it is unlikely that you would trust someone you don't like to make major decisions about your life. If you don't like who you are, allowing yourself to take chances and challenge your boundaries is next to impossible.

Your potential is only as limited as your belief in yourself.

While we can achieve a lot together, you won't be able to truly unlock your potential if you have false beliefs and negative self-labels weighing you down. If I hadn't already started on my journey to self-acceptance, I would never have been able to elevate my career when I experienced my career wake-up call. I wouldn't be writing this book because my inner critic would tell me that what I have to say doesn't matter. *Your inner critic is a liar.*

3. Intentionality

To have the right growth atmosphere, you must shift from thinking, feeling, and acting in a habitual manner to an intentional one. Intentionality is the difference between reacting and responding, between drifting along the river of life in your canoe versus paddling the darn thing. Even *amoebas* react to their environment—you can do better! You can think; you can respond. You have the power of choice over how you interact with changing circumstances.

As you learn and grow, it will require intentional focus on your part to create new habits. Every healthy human brain has what scientists call *neuroplasticity*. Neuroplasticity is the hope for humankind. It is the ability to create new neural pathways and form new habits. It may come as no surprise that new habits are shaped with repetition and practice, both of which are a result of intentional application.

Because so many of these internal atmosphere attributes are intertwined, the impetus to become intentional is sharper once you realize how much of an impact you truly have in your life *and over other people.* Ignoring your influence is what those with fixed mindsets do, and that can lead to chaos.

You might be amazed at just how oblivious we are to our impact on the world. For example, I was in the checkout line at the grocery store one day and behind someone who was talking on their phone. I noticed that they never paused their conversation once to exchange any words with the cashier; they just kept right on talking. It's like the cashier didn't even exist. The expression on the cashier's face revealed that he thought this person was a complete jerk.

When it was my turn to check out, I looked at the cashier, smiled, and said: "I hope you had a great weekend!" I then asked him if he'd done anything fun and how his day was going. These are truly simple things and they cost me nothing. What mattered is that I was *intentional* about them. The cashier's face transformed as we talked, and he looked much happier when I left the store. **You have much more impact than you give yourself credit for—be responsible with it.**

- Ask yourself the following questions:
- How intentional are you?
- What do you *want* to act and think like?
- What are the demonstrated behaviors of that type of person?
- What are your behaviors now?
- Do they align with who you want to be?
- What do you need to do to close the gap?

Being intentional requires you to be present, aware, and in the moment. In order to increase your influence and impact, you must become more observant of your attitude, thoughts, actions, and words. You can choose how to respond to your environment. Don't be an amoeba; be intentional.

4. People-First Focus

In order to see real progress in your career growth, you have to come to grips with the fact that other people matter. It's not about you and how great you are. It's about how other people perceive your actions and words. Sometimes that's a hard pill to swallow. Perception management and your professional presence is key to your career success.

One of the very first rules that I absorbed during my Leadership Psychology training from Cornell was about the mindset shift required to leverage strategic influence. When we think of influence, we are prone to consider what other people can do for *us*. That mindset is backwards. **In order to leverage strategic influence, we have to consider what other people value *first*.**

In order to learn what others value, you have to listen to them. Intentional listening is a skill that can be learned, but it does not come naturally. People find it difficult to focus on what others are saying for any length of time before their internal narrative kicks in. We become so busy with either thinking about what we are going to say or something else entirely that we rarely listen fully to others. Sometimes your internal narrative gets in the way.

Let's take Max, for example. He has a PhD and is super smart. Max came to me confused as to why his education and credentials didn't automatically land him a promotion. It quickly became obvious that his colleagues didn't trust him and some didn't even like him. During our work together, we learned that Max had a habit of being a smart aleck and cuttingly sarcastic. He figured that everyone else couldn't measure up to *him*. Max did not put people first because, until our coaching sessions together, he didn't realize that other people could add any value to his life. He thought he was smarter and, therefore, superior in some way.

When the mistaken logic behind this thought process was revealed, Max was a bit sheepish. He had allowed himself to fall into a very bad habit of devaluing others' contributions just because they weren't what *he* would have said. He also never asked for help (even when he needed it) because he didn't understand the value in collaboration. Max thought he needed to come up with answers on his own, like taking tests in college. The good news is that his colleagues no longer think he's a jerk. Today, he is much more likeable, open-minded, and on the fast-track to leadership.

You do not grow your career in a vacuum. Your success largely depends on other people's perception of your behavior. When we communicate, for example, we often get this concept wrong. Effective communication isn't derived by you conveying a message to someone else. *Effective communication happens only when the other person receives your message the way it is intended.* In other words, you have to communicate with the other person in mind.

Here are my five shifts to becoming more people-focused:

1. **Don't be so judgmental.** No one crowned you King/Queen of Critics. Don't forget that everyone has a diverse way of thinking and a different life experience than you do. Judging others based on our own mental point of reference is a bit, well, silly.
2. **Embrace differences.** Not everyone is just like you, and that's good. It brings variety and beautiful diversity to the world. You can learn so much from other people, *especially* the ones you don't like. The more someone irritates you, the more likely it is that they are a reflection of your own hang-ups.
3. **Shift communication styles.** Communication is about other people, not about you. Often, we are so intent on communicating something that we forget that it's meaningless if the other person doesn't get it. Communicate with other people in mind. How do they need to hear your message based on their perspective and work style?
4. **Perception matters.** Your credibility is owned by you, but it isn't decided by you. Whether you are credible or not relies on other people's perception of who you are. With that in mind, be aware of your words and actions. How will they make other people feel? The point is not to become a people-pleaser, but to be aware and appreciative of others.
5. **Give more.** The more you give, the more you receive. There is a strong universal norm to return a favor, repay a debt, or make a concession. It's a

counterintuitive universal law backed by science: the Law of Reciprocity. However, the effective results of paying things forward work best if you give without expectation of return.

Creating Your Growth Atmosphere

When you embark on your journey of growth to elevate your career, ask yourself, "What of these four focus items do I need more of to be successful?" It is not necessary that you attempt to master each area before you tackle an intentional plan of self-development. As you have probably already noted, many of the transformations myself and my clients have achieved do not require major changes.

Focus on small, yet specific changes to empower radical positive change. If you have an atmosphere for growth in place, you do not need to make sweeping changes. This will conserve the energy you invest in your transformation. Consider what area could use more attention: a growth mindset, self-appreciation, intentionality, or having a people-first focus. It is likely that you will have impressive results just by increasing your awareness in any of these areas.

It is also likely that you want *more* than just these positive changes in your career and your life. You want to elevate your career! You want more impact and income! This is exciting, so let's get started with the tools and techniques you need to ensure that you are directing your attention to the small, yet specific areas of growth that will yield big results.

Chapter 4: Getting Started

"Growth means change. Change requires challenging the status quo. Achievers refuse to accept the status quo."
– John C. Maxwell

You Can't Grow What You Don't Know

It's time to take the blindfold off and start to develop an understanding of who you really are and how others perceive you so you can elevate your career efficiently. To begin, you need to understand what is actually holding you back from seeing the career results you want. *You cannot grow something you don't know.*

Here's a myth-buster for you: career growth has less to do with your technical expertise and more to do with your personal growth. We often have it backwards. We think we can focus on ourselves *after* we grow our career. As a result, this false belief fosters negative workplace environments in our companies and corporate cultures. When people are oblivious to their influence on others, it's easy for the workplace culture to go sour. When leaders value results more than people, they cannot create a people-first culture.

If most people worked on themselves just as hard as they worked at being good at their job, we would have less toxic workplace environments. Sadly, this just isn't the case yet. The vast majority of people are unaware that self-development is important. Most also have the false belief that they cannot change. This is scientifically incorrect.

Because you picked up this book and you are reading this chapter, you already have a good start in the right direction. You have probably already had a few "aha" moments! I have great news for you: this chapter is where you begin the process of removing your roadblocks to get real results.

Becoming the Best Version of You

As I've said before, the "phoenix rising" approach sounds dramatic and awe-inspiring. In reality, there is no reason to totally reinvent yourself. First, this takes an incredible amount of time and energy. Second, it's just not feasible. There are many aspects of yourself that you cannot and *should not* change. These include characteristics that make you unique, honor your gifts, leverage your strengths, and give you the ability to achieve the results you want in your career and in your life.

You can accomplish a tremendous amount of transformation with a few specific shifts in your behavior. No one is asking you to suddenly become someone you are not. That would be incredibly ill-advised. Authenticity is crucial! **Most of the behaviors that get in our way and stagnate our careers are habits that make us *inauthentic*.**

After my pivot point, I felt more freedom to be myself than ever before. For many of us, we are locked into certain ways of thinking, communicating, and behaving because we think we *should* be this way. In order to succeed, I was convinced I shouldn't be social at work even though I'm a very social person. This was inauthentic behavior for me. All of these myths that keep you stuck also encourage behaviors that are often not truly who you are.

If you feel like you have to wear a certain persona to work every day, you know what I mean. For some people, the career myths that keep them stuck also encourage other more natural habits which are not beneficial in the long term. For example, I'm extremely results-oriented. In balance, this is great. However, when combined with an overachieving personality, it can become an issue.

It's absolutely essential to learn exactly what habits you need to let go of so you can achieve your highest potential and elevate your career. Farshad Asl has been known to say: "Knowledge is learning something new every day. Wisdom is letting go of some bad habits every day."

In order to get real results right away, it's imperative that we understand exactly what your biggest roadblocks are. Working on yourself is always a great idea and you will see positive change even if you just pick one thing to work on without definitive data. *Transformational* change only occurs when you remove the biggest barriers to achieving your potential based on definitive data.

When you just grab at anything and begin, you may not have a catalyst for transformational growth. If you don't see the results you desire and receive feedback on your changes relatively quickly, it's easy to become discouraged. In addition, if you feel like there are too many options, it could be overwhelming.

Without more definitive data through feedback and qualified guidance, I've seen clients suffer from analysis paralysis. With too many choices, they were worried that they'd pick the "wrong" thing to work on. After an empathy coaching session, I was able to help them see a path and a framework to achieve their goals.

Get Started on Your Growth Journey

While the steps to discover what you need to let go of aren't mysterious, they can be intimidating to some. After all, change is scary at first. It is perfectly normal to feel a little nervous because new things can be uncomfortable. Acknowledge the discomfort, stick with the process, and you will get results. Habits are hard to change for a reason. I will reveal more about that reason in the coming chapters and give you a means by which to make change easy.

If you feel stuck or that you might be holding yourself back, I encourage you to revisit Chapter 3: The Atmosphere to Fuel Growth. You can achieve transformational change in a very short period of time. Growth requires the right fertilizer, and you do not need to be perfect to get results! However, awareness and the desire to change are necessary to see success with the next steps.

There are three very important things you must keep in mind to get started:

1. Negative feedback does not make you a bad person.
2. Even the tiniest bit of feedback *feels* much larger than it is.
3. The important part of your journey is a willingness to change.

Two essential reminders:

- Driven, experienced women are typically harsher on themselves when receiving feedback. What I see in my driven female clients is a desire to be near perfect in all aspects. Please be kind to yourself. Do not try and "fix" everything that you don't score 100% on! Think about how you can strategically choose a specific roadblock to tackle first. The purpose isn't to be perfect; it is to become incrementally better.
- Conversely, driven, experienced men often struggle to accept that they should change at all. Being open to change does not mean that you are a failure. Developing yourself is an incredibly smart move. Ignoring opportunities for growth will hurt you later on. The cost of ignoring self-development and perception management is more impactful the higher you rise. By growing yourself, you will be better able

Erin Urban

to leverage strategic relationships and elevate your career.

The best data to remove your real roadblocks comes from other people, often in the form of feedback. Feedback can be found through various methods. In order to have a full spectrum of your true career roadblocks, the following tools and people will aid you:

- 360° reviews
- Surveys
- Mentors
- Trusted colleagues
- Family and friends
- Adversaries

Feedback Methods Overview

360° reviews are arguably the best and most informative method to elicit feedback from those you work with. Ideally, your workplace will already have some form of feedback tool in use by your human resources department. If appropriate, you can connect with your HR representative to get help in deploying the tool.

From time to time, either my client's organization does not have a tool and/or they are not open to the use of a third-party resource. If you are not able to use a formal 360° review, don't worry, there are other methods to help you get the necessary feedback. I will review the best one in the next chapter.

Surveys are the easiest method to gain insights into your career roadblocks. However, there are a few important challenges with deploying a survey. You have to make sure it is a "blind" survey. In other words, you send the survey to the people you want feedback from, but you do not collect their emails.

In order to get good feedback, you have to create anonymity. Otherwise, it's unlikely that people will be honest with you because they don't want you to be mad at them. That's how we are wired.

Mentors are incredibly important in anyone's professional development and can provide great insights. However, not everyone has the luxury of having a great mentor available. Keep in mind that your mentor is only one person and you may need more than one point of view.

Mentors are very helpful when you need to debrief the feedback you have received. It's valuable to have another person's objective perspective. Feedback is emotional and there are several phases to receiving it. I will have more detail about this in the next chapter.

Trusted colleagues and family/friends can be sources of guidance as well. However, it's likely that you may not get a raw and honest appraisal because they don't want to upset you. They may give you a diplomatic answer, but most won't be extremely blunt because they may be worried that it will damage your relationship. While it is perfectly fine to reach out to those you are closest to, you may need to establish expectations first.

Your adversaries can be great sources of feedback if they are open to speaking with you and they are credible. The viability of this method depends on the personality type of your adversary. Most of us know people at work that we don't necessarily see eye-to-eye with. Whether you can leverage this person depends on how abrasive the relationship is and the nature of your discord.

If your adversary is someone who you feel would sabotage you, then *do not* leverage this person for feedback. It's likely the information you will receive is worthless or designed to hurt you intentionally. If your adversary has a gap in their work ethic or moral code, do not engage them in this process. On the other hand, if this person exhibits great work ethics and is morally sound but you just don't get along, then they could be a good resource. Use your best judgement here.

Why Most People Fail to Get Results

You may have already decided to work on several different challenges from the previous chapters, but you don't have all the data yet! Even the most self-aware person just simply does not have enough information (based on an outside perspective) to have a concrete idea of where to start. When it comes to receiving insights into how you are perceived, you need to involve those around you. You don't see yourself in action, and you aren't the recipient of your own behaviors; other people are.

The good news is that it's not hard or mysterious to enlist support and get good feedback on where you need to grow. Even if you don't want to invest in a formal analysis like a 360° review, there are various methods and means by which to get great information and target your first growth goal.

On the other hand, if you try to close gaps you *think* are issues without getting feedback, you may not see any real results. More often than not, what I see are well-meaning professionals who take only one piece of random information or one circumstance and decide to fix the problem. Sometimes it pays off. After all, some growth is better than none (or so we think). Other times, it results in a clear miss or complete confusion.

With the clear miss examples, I have seen them take well-rounded feedback too harshly and it resulted in personality suppression and ineffectuality. By going solo and trying to change without any structure, training, or expert guidance, you can create more problems than you solve. If you want to elevate your career to see exponential results quickly, then you need more data and you need a structure. This is what this book is all about!

Let's take Tom, for instance. When Tom first came to me, he was frustrated at his lack of career results. After receiving strong feedback that he was too aggressive in his work style, he attempted to solve the problem. Unfortunately, he went too far and completely suppressed his personality. He went from being Tom the Tiger to Tom the Timid. He stopped seeing the results he used to enjoy. While those results were admittedly at the expense of other people, he now felt like he couldn't get anything right and his self-esteem was in the ditch.

No one paid him any real attention anymore and he felt sidelined. His career was stagnating and he said to me at our first meeting: "I feel like I'm darned if I do or darned if I don't." Tom didn't feel like he could be himself, so he became nothing. People didn't take him seriously because Tom didn't take *himself* seriously. He wasn't sure what to do, but he knew what he was doing wasn't getting him the results he needed to elevate his career.

By our second meeting, I could see serious changes in Tom. We worked together to dive into the real roadblocks (largely self-confidence based), and he began to grow. In less than 60 days, he was given a critical strategic project where he could practice his newfound skills and build relationships better than ever before. A few months after that project was completed, Tom was chosen for a managerial role and put on the path to senior leadership.

Tom needed more clarity, better data, and a framework to get to the *real* root of his true roadblocks and find his authentic self. What's so amazing about the transformation process is that you are not becoming someone you aren't; rather, you are unlocking your full potential. **You become the best version of *you*.**

Chapter 5: Identify Your Roadblocks

"It's so important to reach out to people you trust, and who can give you honest feedback, and keep those people close to you. You don't want to surround yourself with enablers."
-Tim Gunn

Let's dive into exactly how to leverage the tools and methods outlined in the previous section. In order to get results in a short period of time, these next steps and the following chapters are essential to your success. If you are not enlisting the help of a qualified professional to debrief your feedback, I recommend that you leverage more than one method to aid your first steps.

360° Reviews

The 360° review is the gold standard in my coaching practice. Marshall Goldsmith, a leading executive behavioral coach, said in his book, *What Got You Here Won't Get You There*: "[Feedback is] the only tool I need to show people, 'You Are Here'."[4]

---

[4] Marshall Goldsmith, *What Got You Here Won't Get You There* (Hachette Books, 2014), 8.

Feedback can be incredibly powerful if facilitated and delivered properly.

The challenge with most feedback is that it is a "lagging indicator", doesn't always ask the right questions, and (if not managed correctly) can do more harm than good. On the other hand, some feedback is better than none. In my corporate years, I participated in and received plenty of formalized feedback reviews. Only one had the power of transformational change and, to be honest, it was facilitated poorly. **It's often not the feedback itself that's helpful;** *it's how you receive the feedback that matters.*

My pivot point could have been more powerful if the feedback had been properly given, but it wasn't. As a result, it took me longer to set my growth goals. If I had a qualified facilitator to debrief me, the immediate result would have been much different. It's not uncommon to receive constructive or critical feedback and then think it was a load of baloney. Feedback often isn't accepted very well based on who it was delivered by, how it was given, and/or how much emotion the feedback was based on.

Take my pivot point for example: my feedback was from someone who I didn't like or respect. Their delivery of the information was almost guaranteed to infuriate me. To make matters worse, some of the examples given of my "bad" behaviors were over six months old. This was not the best scenario to encourage me to take the critique seriously. If it hadn't been for the fortunate triangulation of other influences, the feedback may have missed the mark entirely and I wouldn't be where I am today.

- **Engaged feedback is more effective.** In other words, you *ask* for an analysis; it isn't thrust upon you. It is easy to get defensive when we receive unwanted feedback, even if it's valuable for our growth. Instead of thinking "I need to look into this", you start creating reasons why the criticism isn't true or worth considering.
- **Feedback methods and tools matter.** Not all feedback tools are created equal. Some have different drivers, whether they be behavioral based, EI (EQ) based, or performance based, among others. Be sure to choose a tool that is *behavioral* based. Otherwise, you may have a very difficult time interpreting the data into something useful.
- **Focus on your lowest scores.** Most 360° review products have a scoring system. Being "rated" can incite a feeling of alarm if you don't achieve the score you expected. By obsessing about this, it's easy to get discouraged and/or distracted when you need to focus on the items that have the lowest score *only*. For example, let's say that the rating scale is from 0–5. You score 4.6 on one item and it shocks you because you thought you should be a complete 5. It's easy to get derailed and ignore an item that was only 2.4, but you *expected* it to be low. *Even if you expected it, focus on the lowest rating!*

- **Trust is important to avoid feedback failures.** Make
sure that the person facilitating the feedback is
someone you trust and respect. If this is not the case,
it's likely that your natural defensiveness will surface
and you may not take the critique seriously. You could
get so caught up in the delivery that you miss the
importance of what is being said. In *Thanks for the
Feedback*, by Douglas Stone and Sheila Heen, they call
this a "Relationship Trigger." They state that: "Our
focus shifts from the feedback itself to the audacity of
the person delivering it."[5]

The great thing about formal 360° reviews is the anonymity
of the responders. Responders are the people who are giving
you feedback. If you get caught up in who said what, not only
is that unproductive, it can damage the review experience to the
point of stagnation. Think of it like this: how likely is it that you
will accept feedback from someone you think isn't "qualified"
to give it? What if a close colleague gives you constructive
criticism, but it doesn't fit with your self-identity?

Instead of bogging you down in an overly emotional,
counterproductive, and arguably negative experience,
anonymous feedback allows you to absorb the reported data
more freely. You aren't worried about who said what and why;

---

[5] Douglas Stone and Sheila Heen, *Thanks for the Feedback* (Penguin Books, 2015), 16.

you can focus on the key takeaways. Also, your respondents can rest easy that you won't be gunning for them later.

Enlist Support With 360° Reviews

If you decide to go out on your own with a formal 360° review, it may be more challenging. If you want to see results fast and you want to use one of the comprehensive 360° review products to elicit feedback, then get support during this process. Because I've been on both sides of the growth experience as a coach and as a person being coached, I strongly recommend that you get guidance in the form of a mentor or, ideally, a qualified professional to debrief any formalized critique.

Without the proper training, it can be difficult to interpret the results from a structured assessment into an action plan for personal development and career growth. Without fail, in every single one of my clients' debriefing sessions, I share insights that surprise them. This is not because I have mysterious magical powers. I have the training and years of expertise that enable me to see the results from a completely unique and insightful perspective.

I also understand how to help my clients navigate the phases of feedback. When we receive criticism, we often go through phases comparable to the grief cycle, as pioneered by Elizabeth Kübler-Ross.[6] Her model states that people will experience

---

[6] "Kübler-Ross model," Wikipedia, *https://en.wikipedia.org/wiki/K%C3%BCbler-Ross_model.*

denial, anger, depression/contemplation, bargaining, and acceptance. In the business context, while most people may not experience all of the phases, it largely depends on how misaligned the feedback is with our self-identity.

Our response to feedback is *always* emotional first, not logical. Logic comes after contemplation. Without the right guidance through the process, sometimes we allow emotion to drive our cognitive function and we come to the completely wrong conclusion. Keep in mind that none of these assessments I have mentioned have anything to do with your potential, IQ, abilities, or have any bearing on how good a person you are.

The point of these tools and methods is to shed light on what is actually hurting your career growth potential versus what you *think* it is. If you are reasonably self-aware, you may have an idea about your potential roadblocks or maybe you've already had some constructive feedback. What is concerning to me, as a coaching professional, is that there was a time when I thought I was self-aware—and I clearly missed the mark. Get qualified guidance!

Creating Feedback Surveys

Surveys are cheaper and perhaps easier to use, but sometimes they are not anonymous. You can create surveys that do not collect email addresses and provide a web link to collect information. With personal security being a huge focus, it's important to give those participating in your survey peace of mind. It's also important for *you*. The good news is that there are an increasing number of free survey tools that allow customization and large numbers of respondents.

The downside to surveys is that you need to set up and establish the questions. Unless this is facilitated by a professional, it's likely you might miss key questions. One of the challenges is to ensure response consistency and accuracy. It's also extremely helpful to have the data debriefed by a professional to aid you in discovering exactly what to focus on first. Because surveys are easier and cheaper (and, therefore, more likely to be used), I have resources on my website for anyone that has this book. You can access basic questions to help you gather better quality data.

Basic survey questions and resources can be found at www.coacheurban.com – under the 'Books' tab or at www.elevateyourcareerbook.com

Connecting with Mentors

Some of the most successful people in business have mentors. As a career coach, I can say that mentors have made all the difference in my career development. Mentors helped inspire, guide, and shape the person I am today. I firmly believe that without key influencers assisting me in my pivot point, I would not have been able to secure a leadership role. Because the right people intervened at the right time, I was able to reap the rewards from a powerful mentoring relationship and elevate my career.

John Maxwell says, "If you want to go fast, go alone. If you want to go far, take others with you."[7] There is a lot of truth in this. Only the very arrogant or ignorant shun the unique insight that comes from partnering with the right mentor. Life's lessons are best learned from others. **Finding the right mentor could make the difference between floundering in your professional career or making it big.**

A mentor can challenge, inform, connect, and inspire you. I spent many wasted years in my youth trying to bushwhack through the professional jungle alone. I was fiercely independent and determined that I could find the right answers by myself. For some reason, I thought asking for guidance was a weakness. I see now that I was a fool. Fortunately, someone saw past my stubbornness and gave me a chance to benefit from a mentoring relationship.

Not all mentors are made equal and not every successful professional can help you make a leap forward professionally. The knowledge and wisdom gained from a solid mentoring relationship are not found with just anyone. The following are proven insights to ensure that you find the best mentor to elevate your career:

1. Avoid being star-struck. Do not ask an idol to be a mentor. If you are in awe of someone, chances are you will not be in the mental position necessary to retain the important information

---

[7] Shila Morris, "Are You Really a Team Leader?" The John Maxwell Team, *https://johnmaxwellteam.com/are-you-really-a-team-leader/*.

your mentor provides. Your brain will be too busy comparing your experience to your expectations. You may not feel comfortable openly asking questions or even being yourself.

2. Define your idea of success. A successful mentoring relationship starts with someone you can look up to professionally. Clearly define what your idea of success looks like for your career focus. This will help guide you to find the right mentor. A professional who has proven success in their career and the experience to impart knowledge will be in a better position to aid you towards your goals.

3. Experience matters. Mentors cannot give what they don't have. Inexperienced individuals will struggle to become successful mentors. Mentoring relationships with peers tend to be shorter and more narrowly focused. These can be beneficial if approached correctly. Mentoring relationships established with more experienced professionals usually allow the mentee to access additional knowledge depth.

4. Seek unbiased support. A good mentor is someone who is fulfilled in what they do, is professionally successful, and has no vested interest in where you go in your career. A good mentor will only be interested in lifting you up and giving you the tools needed to succeed regardless of your path.

5. Be specific on the why. Define and explain why you approached a particular professional to be your mentor. As the mentee, you have everything to gain. The mentor is donating time and attention to you. You must have a tangible and specific reason why you asked someone to mentor you. The fact that they make a lot of money is not the most compelling reason to choose a mentor.

6. Communicate your goal. What does a successful mentoring relationship outcome look like to you, and what specifically do you want to learn? Clearly communicate what your goal is from the partnership and why you are sure that your mentor can get you there.

7. Be prepared. As a mentee, you have a job to do. In addition to being a sponge, soaking up all the knowledge you can, you must also be prepared for each mentoring session. Best practices are:

- Take notes during each session.
- Determine actionable items at the end of a session.
- Be prepared to report on what you applied from the last session.
- Have questions ready ahead of time for your mentor.

A powerful mentoring relationship between two professionals can be mutually beneficial. The mentor also gains insight during the act of coaching another professional. When it comes to aiding you with specific developmental feedback, a mentor is an invaluable resource. You can also enlist a mentor to help you unpack the results of any do-it-yourself surveys you created. An unbiased and objective perspective is incredibly powerful in your growth journey. It also limits our natural tendency to dwell in the status quo, ruminate, and basically drag our feet instead of getting started!

Any professional who strives for solo victories will discover that the road to success is rocky. It's nice to have a helping hand over the hurdles. It took me valuable years to understand that a solid mentoring partnership can clear the path to success. If you want to truly elevate your career and achieve your potential, I encourage you to develop a vision of the fulfilling future you desire and reach out to a mentor to help you along the way.

Trusted Colleagues, Friends, and Family

In the absence of 360° reviews, surveys, and mentors, enlisting the help of your support community can be a great place to start. While the data sample size will be more restricted, you will at least get some idea where to begin. However, use this path with caution. It may be challenging to achieve unbiased results from people you know and love.

For example, while my mother is usually very straightforward with me, I am still surprised to learn that she doesn't think I'm ready to hear all the brutal truth about myself. From time to time, those who are closest to you can be just as blind as you are to your blind spots! Just like my mom, they may seek to protect you from yourself. They don't want to hurt your feelings and they certainly don't wish to damage your relationship. While well-meaning, this isn't very helpful when it comes to making specific and significant changes in order to see the results you want.

Also, not everyone that knows you sees you in action at work. Sometimes it's possible to enlist the aid of your fellow colleagues in your endeavors to improve. It is also human nature to hedge our bets and only reveal a portion of the truth to someone in order to avoid angering them.

For example, a client, Sam, really wanted to know why it seemed like he was always passed up for promotions and opportunities to rise into upper management. He'd achieved middle management, but he was hungry for more. Sam was ambitious, smart, mentally agile, and very insightful, but if you met him and didn't know him well, you would have no idea that he was so capable—not right away.

The only reason I had any idea was because, as a coach, it's my business to ask nosey questions and help my clients discover more about themselves. During our second session, I shared with him: "The biggest reason you aren't seeing the career opportunities you want has nothing to do with your ability to deliver results." After further coaching, Sam realized his roadblock was his *voice*. His soft-spoken demeanor made people think that he wasn't self-confident. His presence wasn't in alignment with his abilities! I helped him see that he needed to project his voice and allow his internal confidence to shine through. Sam's tone of voice and body language were killing his career growth.

Thanks to my action-oriented approach to help Sam unlock his potential, he landed the opportunity he really wanted. His colleagues, he reported, were a little shocked at first, but quickly warmed to the new (and still authentic) Sam. It's important to note here that the adjustments he made had nothing to do with reinventing himself.

When you are seeking to remove career roadblocks, remember that:

- You don't have to become someone you aren't.
- You have to identify and remove your biggest roadblocks *first*.
- You will be amazed how powerful small, yet significant, shifts can be to unlock your potential!

Leveraging Your Adversaries

From time to time, you can leverage broken relationships to make big changes. Most of us have someone that we just simply don't get along with. Because this person may not see eye-to-eye with you, they may provide more direct feedback than someone who you consider a good friend. Basically, that's because they aren't afraid of damaging the relationship if it's already broken.

Use this method with caution. If you feel that your adversary has questionable morals or would intentionally sabotage you, then don't bother. Extensive emotional involvement can also cloud good results. Trust your instincts and use your best judgement here. Also, if the relationship is too rocky, your adversary might not even want to talk to you. However, if you feel that this person is of sound ethical character, they may be a good resource if they are willing.

Sometimes, you can get feedback without asking for it explicitly. If you would like to attempt to repair your relationship with this person, then this is a great gateway to having a more in-depth conversation about what the challenges might be. The caveat here is that the dialogue must focus on what *you* can do to repair the situation, not enumerate what they have done to you. If you wish to take this route and feel that your adversary may have good insights for you, here are some tips:

- Make sure you express that hearing their point of view is important to you.
- Establish that you desire for them to be candid with you.
- Meet with them in person at a place of their choosing. No phone calls. Video meetings are an option only if there are geographical constraints.
- Express your intent to understand how you can improve the relationship.
- Listen with intent and silence your internal dialogue.
- Listen longer than you normally would. Often, people may add more information past the natural pause.
- Clarify what you heard to ensure accuracy of the message; seek to gain understanding.
- Do not justify, excuse, or explain anything in your defense. If they express something that is not true, you can say: "I'm sorry to hear that you felt that way."
- When they are finished sharing, ask: "Is that everything?"
- When they are completely done, reiterate what they said and then ask: "Do you feel that I understand?"
- If there are any actions you feel that you can legitimately take, express them.

- Ask if you can follow up with them to gain feedback on your progress. Be prepared to hear the word "No."
- Thank them for their time and express your desire to seek common ground for a better future working relationship.

Occasionally, you will run across blatant falsehoods. If you absolutely need to clarify the truth for a compelling reason, be cautious in how you approach the subject. Word choice is very important. You can say: "May I express the scenario from my understanding?" Or: "Are you open to hearing an alternate viewpoint that may illuminate the situation?"

Take Action

As an action-oriented coach, I encourage you to pick one method of obtaining feedback and *get started*. You need to know what your biggest roadblock is so you can get transformational results. I have shared that a 360° review is the gold standard in my coaching practice. Even so, that does not rule out any of the other methods for getting feedback.

We are naturally change-averse creatures. We gravitate to our comfort zones and will stay there as long as possible. The problem is that although a comfort zone is a beautiful place, nothing ever grows there. Most people simply allow their lives to happen to them. We float along; we react. By the time a great portion of our lives has passed, we wake up to the realization that we should have been more proactive. We spend more time planning our next vacation than our careers.

The reason we don't focus on planning our career growth is because we tend to be misguided by career growth myths that we think should empower a career uplift. Additionally, many people don't believe in themselves. **If you don't believe in yourself or if you think success is automatic, it's not likely that you will give your career the attention it deserves.**

What's sad is how many people need clarity in their lives, but don't know that they can change. You don't have to accept the status quo. Thanks to new discoveries in neuroscience, the myth that adults cannot change their mindset or behavior has been erased. Also, you do not have to make revolutionary changes to see outstanding results. In fact, my clients are constantly amazed at how transformational small changes can be!

It's time to realize that you *can* change and unlock your potential. It's time to give yourself the keys to elevate your career.

Chapter 6: Remove Your Roadblocks

"Without change, something sleeps inside us, and seldom awakens. The sleeper must awaken."
- Frank Herbert

What To Do With Your Feedback

You've got feedback, you reviewed the results with an informed professional, and you are ready to get started. You may have used a 360° review, a survey, a mentor, your colleagues, or even enlisted the aid of your friends and family. Perhaps you are an overachiever and did everything! The big question is: now what?

I find that most driven professionals want to tackle everything. I highly recommend that you do not attempt to focus on too much at once. If you used a 360° review, pick your lowest ratings even if these did not surprise you. Within those lowest ratings you may find that you have one mindset opportunity, one behavioral, and one strategic.

If that seems like a lot (and you want get results right away), pick only *one* behavioral challenge to focus on first. I will discuss in more detail how to streamline the process by targeting a single habit in Chapter 8: Fast-Track Your Growth.

Processing Your Feedback

When I was working with my client Mary on her career growth plan, she was overwhelmed by the 360° review feedback at first. She went through the typical phases: denial (while saying, "I'm not denying the facts" about 15 times), deflection, reflection, and, finally, acceptance. Guidance from a certified coach through the initial phases of a feedback debrief will help you achieve more effective results. Qualified support will help you process the feedback without falling into a negative thinking loop or succumbing to denial.

Feedback isn't always pleasant to hear. We all have an identity we've created for ourselves. When your self-beliefs are challenged, it's normal to feel defensive. It is important to process, ask questions, and sometimes adjust to the shock of having to realign your self-identity with reality. The feedback you receive may be a rude awakening. It certainly was for me during my fateful performance review that was my catalyst for change.

Even well-intentioned but poorly presented feedback offers you an opportunity to grow. If the critique challenges your sense of self, your ego may get in the way, encouraging you to become bitter instead of better. When something challenges your belief structure, it's natural to deny that it might be true. However, when you are aware that this will happen, it gives you a fighting chance to push your ego aside to see if there is an opportunity for improvement.

Once Mary processed the feedback with my support and arrived at the acceptance stage; it wasn't surprising that she immediately wanted to work on areas she thought she should have scored better on from her 360° review, rather than the lowest ratings. Fortunately, I had primed her by setting the expectation that we would only be focusing on the items that received the lowest ratings and go from there.

Mary's immediate inclination to focus on what she thought should be perfect is a common reaction. I find that most experienced professionals have some idea what their roadblocks might be; they just aren't aware that it's an issue. It's a part of who you are, and you don't question it. You may even recognize, on some level, that it can be annoying to others. Yet you may not actually find any real reason to change because you've *identified* with your bad habit. The problem is, it's still a bad habit!

Your Top Three Transformation Targets

In Mary's case, she was next in line for a big promotion. This promotion would either be given to her or another senior leader at her level. Her lowest score resulted from her tendency to "vent" her feelings when she got frustrated. She wasn't surprised to learn she had this habit; she was only guilty of ignoring her impact. Mary didn't stop to think that when she vented, it caused additional stress for her team.

Item #1 on her action plan was to tackle this behavioral issue. Item #2 was a mindset shift. It became apparent in our work together that she didn't feel like she was a leader. She just got stuff done and managed people. It's not that Mary didn't acknowledge her role; she didn't think of herself in terms of senior leadership. This resulted in behavior that was more manager-like. Her granular approach held her back from embracing that she is, in fact, a senior leader, not just a manager. This was confirmed in the feedback she received.

Making the distinction between a management and a leadership mindset was incredibly important for her. The seemingly subtle mindset shift allowed Mary to spot some key behaviors like poor word choice, tone of voice, and unfortunate facial expressions that held her firmly under the top leadership strata. Once she elevated her self-awareness to that of a senior leader, she let go of behaviors that no longer served her. Mary was then able to fine tune her executive presence and develop the perceptions that were in line with her career goals.

Item #3 had to do with strategy. Whether you are a leader or not, if you want to grow your career, you need to be strategic about it. Mary had expressed early on that she felt constantly overwhelmed. "I can't get anything accomplished because people keep popping into my office and bugging me," she said. During the feedback debrief, it was obvious that her peers saw her as super busy and having too much on her plate. It also became clear that her managers felt like they should check in with her on things that she'd rather they solved on their own.

At first pass, this may seem pretty normal for anyone in a management role, particularly for someone who had a reputation for getting stuff done. The problem was that she was drowning in work and hadn't quite mastered the art of delegation or leveraging her allies. She needed to enlist support at her level, to learn to say "no" to non-value-add busy work, and to empower her team to solve problems on their own. By implementing key tactics, Mary was able to extract herself from feeling overburdened and was no longer pulled in a zillion directions at once.

Mary's new strategic focus freed her to tackle opportunities leading to senior leadership. Also, as a bonus, her team got the chance to step up, solve problems within their control, and release their dependency on her constant guidance. As a result, this sent signals to Mary's chain of command that she was capable of delegation *and* staff development, not just management. By thinking like the leader she is, Mary increased her influence at the senior executive level.

Tackling Your Top Three Targets

When you are tackling your top three issues, choose the lowest ratings and go from there. Select a mindset opportunity, a behavioral change, and one item that will help you strategically grow your career. If that sounds like too much, it is also a great idea to stick with only one focus area. **If you choose one aspect to address first, pick a behavioral change that you scored lowest on or got the most feedback to improve on.** Once you pick one item, check out Chapter 8: Fast-Track Your Growth to set up a plan that will get you the most return on your invested energy.

Mindset Focus

To better identify a mindset opportunity, it is important to be able to identify the biggest gaps in your perspective. The challenge here is that our mindset is literally an automatic mental program. We are rarely actively conscious of it. Because we seldom fact-check our mindset, it develops systematic drift over time.

Most of us have a gap between where we are, mentally, and what we want to achieve in our lives. For example, in order to start writing years ago, I had to overcome a mindset rooted in a false belief. My inner critic told me that what I had to say didn't really matter. I had to remind myself that sharing my experiences and knowledge might make a big impact on *someone*. Because of this, I was able to ignore my inner critic and share my knowledge through my writing.

From time to time, an obvious mindset roadblock isn't highlighted in your feedback. This could be simply because the participants don't know you well enough. Alternatively, you might be a more reserved person who shares little. Earlier in this book, I enumerated some of the most common roadblocks I see as a coach and have personally experienced. Did something from that list in Chapter 2 ring a bell?

If you did not receive feedback to help you identify a potential mindset gap, you can ask yourself:

- Based on where you want to go in your career, what do you feel is your biggest mindset roadblock?

- How do you contrast your mindset to those who are in the positions you seek? Do you see any gaps?
- What does your inner critic tell you when you think about elevating your career?
- What type of mindset do you feel would empower you to be better at your work?
- When you consider elevating your career and clearing roadblocks, is your inherent reaction positive or negative? Why?

If you are still stuck, you might want to review what creates the ideal internal growth atmosphere from Chapter 3. Many times, our internal roadblocks are not obvious because our mindset has become our habitual way of being. We don't have to *think* about it. Your mindset is on automatic pilot. I encourage deeper work to discover what mental habits are getting in the way of accomplishing your goals.

For instance, Mary had no conscious idea that she didn't think of herself as a leader until I suggested the possibility to her based on our conversations. She came to a sudden awareness when I asked the question: "Mary, do you genuinely think of yourself as a senior leader or a manager that gets things done?" Up until that moment, it was an automatic mindset that was programmed into her brain, running silently in the background and sabotaging her efforts to embody senior leadership.

Behavioral Focus

Behavioral gaps are usually pretty clear in your feedback. Other people are quick to pick up on exhibited (or missing) behaviors that are not aligned with cultural or social norms and expectations. For example, if you don't listen well to others, they probably know that about you. If you tend to feel like you have to be right or have the last word, other people will pick up on that too. Similarly, if you don't share much and are withdrawn, others will sense this. They may know less about you, but that doesn't mean they haven't made false assumptions about you in the absence of any data - which can present a host of other problems.

Sometimes, you may not have a clear behavioral target. For one of my clients, the feedback was vague and slightly misleading. At first, the critique Trevor received seemed to indicate that he didn't value other people's ideas. That was not the case at all. In fact, he truly loved it when people shared their ideas and he asked for others' input frequently. After some thought and my observations as a coach, we realized that the problem was his body language.

Trevor had a tendency to frown when he was thinking. Even if you knew him very well, you were never quite sure why he was frowning. While Trevor loved ideas, he was more reserved and less inclined to show emotion. He liked to think about things and then circle back. Sometimes he became busy and took even longer to circle back. Occasionally he forgot to touch base altogether.

As a result, his team thought that he didn't value their input, so they shared less. Who wants their manager to frown at them? His peers weren't sure where they stood with him either. Trevor had no notion that he was frowning until I pointed out this body language habit during one of our sessions. I asked him if what I had said was upsetting and he said, "No, of course not. I'm thinking about it." A few questions later, it became clear that the behavior Trevor needed to work on was frowning and timely acknowledgement.

On occasion, the data you receive from your feedback needs a little research to understand exactly where it is coming from. It is not always something you can take at face value. Habits are automatic and they are not something we are always consciously aware of. We judge ourselves by our intentions (which no one can see); other people judge us by our actions, which may not align with our intent!

Strategic Focus

When working to elevate your career, I highly recommend a strategic focus area. This may be obvious in your feedback information. If not, consider your career target and what you want to accomplish. When putting together a career growth plan, start with the end in mind.

By reverse engineering your plan for growth, you are better able to spot exactly where you can be more strategic about your career choices. You may want to pursue particular types of projects, become active in specific professional organizations, connect with industry experts, seek out certain people for mentoring, or even apply for targeted roles that help you get where you want to go.

Busy professionals can suffer from "open door syndrome". They are so absorbed in what they are doing, in their work and their lives, that they just walk through whatever door is open. As a result, you can end up in a job that doesn't fit you, is unfulfilling, or isn't where you wanted to go in the first place. The good news is that there is no time like the present to make a great career plan!

Getting Started On Your Shift

With your top three items in mind, it is important to have a plan to accomplish your goals. This is where I see several, otherwise outstanding, books fall right off the cliff. Many inspiring self-help authors talk a lot about theory, but there's no process to *apply* anything!

I'm a process person. I like lists, steps, and a framework. I have never seen anything truly transformational happen by making wild guesses and taking random actions. Some people achieve marginal success by just doing whatever "feels" right. Unfortunately, the results from random methods rarely stick. I'm not in the marginal success business and I don't recommend an aimless approach to self-improvement. For one, it is incredibly difficult to repeat because there is no method to the madness!

Create Habit Awareness

When it comes to transformational change, it is not enough to just get feedback and superficially understand what your top three targets are. It is very difficult to change habits, and knowing what they are isn't enough. **You must create habit awareness.**

Habits are basically deeply ingrained neural networks. There is a saying in neuroscience that *neurons that fire together, wire together*. The more often you repeat a thought, behavior, or an action, the stronger the response pattern becomes. It takes more effort to do unfamiliar things. Habits exist because your brain likes to save energy and it is indiscriminate about whether or not the behavior itself is useful or even good.

Because habits are like automatic programs running in your mind, it is not enough just to *decide* to change. By becoming acutely aware of what triggers the behavior, how you feel when the behavior is triggered, and the impact of the behavior, you have a better chance of making a sustainable shift.

To make the habit awareness process clearer, I will share a diagnostic tool that I provide to my clients. Most mindset habits are linked to an emotion. This tool allows you to identify and break down your triggers to then reframe your responses into the more effective/positive reaction you desire.

Mindset & Emotion Diagnostic Tool

What triggers the behavior (or mindset)? Is it circumstantial, environmental, a person, a place, or an emotional state? Think about what pushes the "start" button on your behavior. Studies have shown that driving, for example, increases cortisol levels in the blood,[8] an indicator of enhanced stress. This, in turn, can ignite an unfortunate habitual behavior such as tailgating, yelling at traffic, anxiety, and other negative mindset shifts.

What is the emotion? Most of our habitual behaviors are linked to an emotion. Just like an automatic response program, there is a feeling involved when the trigger is activated. What do you feel when your target behavior is triggered? You might notice that you have more than one emotion, such as anxiety and anger. Is there a physical response as well, such as an upset stomach or a headache? Becoming aware of how your body *feels* when the behavior occurs is critical to preemptively identifying the onset of a habit.

What were your initial raw thoughts? Reflect on the situation and quickly jot down your raw emotional thoughts. Do not judge yourself on those immediate responses to a situation, even if they are ugly! It is important to capture the

---

[8] Michael Antoun, Kate M. Edwards, Joanna Sweeting, and Ding Ding, "The acute physiological stress response to driving: A systematic review," *PLoS One* 12, no. 10 (2017): e0185517, *https://www.ncbi.nlm.nih.gov/pmc/articles/PMC5642886/.*

immediate reaction as it is. This is also a great first step in awareness to retrain your mind.

What is the impact? When your habit unleashes itself onto your external or internal world, what happens? What do you notice? For example, if your habit is chronically interrupting people, what changes do you note in their body language, mood, or behavior afterward? This also helps my clients observe the negative impacts on other people in real time, which often speeds up a behavioral shift.

Can you adjust your emotional thoughts/response? This step is essential if you are attempting to rescript a mindset behavior. Review those raw emotional thoughts or assumptions for any distortions. Rewrite them based on facts and what you actually know. Some common distortions are:

- **All-or-nothing thinking.** No grey areas. You are only okay if you make no mistakes. Even one mistake equals abject failure.
- **Overgeneralization.** You draw broad conclusions from one negative event: "I *never* get a parking spot" or "I *never* win anything."
- **Magnification.** You exaggerate difficulties and shortcomings; small problems suddenly become a catastrophe in your mind.
- **Labeling.** Also known as "cussing people out." You attach personality tags to others based on their behaviors: "I can't believe she took the last cookie— she's so greedy!"

- **Ignoring positives.** You filter out positive or dissenting information. If positive information gets through, you downplay it. This is commonly known as "deflecting".
- **Jumping to conclusions.** With little to no data, you immediately leap to the negative interpretation of neutral events. You read others' minds and assume that they think the worst: "Bob didn't return my call; he must be avoiding me."
- **Over-responsibility.** You claim to have omnipotent powers and become responsible for events outside of your control: "I'm in so much trouble. It rained today and that ruined our plans!"

Once you review your raw thoughts and filter out any obvious distortions, your adjusted responses will look vastly different. With repeated practice, you will incite an actual shift in your base emotional response. This practice is very similar to cognitive restructuring.[9]

Keep A Log Or A Journal

Unless you have been gifted with the rare power of perfect memory, I recommend writing things down. Because writing is not everyone's thing, you can do anything from keeping a log on a spreadsheet to a checklist. If you don't mind adding a little

------

[9] "Cognitive restructuring," Wikipedia, https://en.wikipedia.org/wiki/Cognitive_restructuring.

detail, I also recommend a daily journal to elevate your habit awareness.

Every client I work with must log, note, or journal. Otherwise, most attempts at growth and change fail. Awareness happens in the moment and it is fleeting. It is highly unlikely that you will remember pertinent details at the end of the week or even a day later. It is best to make notes while the situation is fresh in your mind. The point is to become acutely aware of *exactly* what triggers your bad habits, so you can circumvent them and shift your mindset.

You are also more likely to see better results when you reflect daily. The power of reflection is vastly underrated and often overlooked. People think you learn through experiences. That's simply not the case; you learn through *evaluated* experiences! We all know someone that keeps repeating the same life experiences over and over again. It seems like they never learn anything so they can move forward.

As a respected colleague of mine, Dr. Rob Pennington, says: "Your personality can be defined by two things: the lessons you have learned and the lessons you haven't learned. All your stress is about an unlearned lesson."[10] By intentionally developing a practice of daily reflection, you can fuel

---

[10] Dr. Rob Pennington, *https://drrobpennington.com/.* LinkedIn: *https://www.linkedin.com/in/robertpenningtonphd/.*

extraordinary mindset transformations because you are accelerating your learning.

Here are three essential questions to ask yourself in your daily journal:

1. What do I have to be grateful for today?

The reason I encourage my clients to begin with an elevated emotion is that it encourages your brain and body to focus on positive things. You are less likely to review a negative laundry list and much more likely to be productive in your journaling practice. Another benefit is that you are training your brain to be more intentionally positive versus reminding yourself of everything that is wrong, not as you expected, or disappointing you.

Elevated emotions discourage us from slipping into negative habitual thought patterns and help us relearn (or rewrite) new neural pathways based on positive feelings. This is not about ignoring anything bad that happens. The purpose is to have a positive action-oriented mindset instead of what I call "negative quicksand" that traps you into a fruitless cycle of misery and self-doubt.

2. What did I learn today?

You have, largely, two choices in your life after an experience (particularly challenging ones): you can get better or bitter. Through this process, I hope that you will choose the first one! **The more you learn your way through life, the less you will**

need to repeat difficult situations. This prepares us to respond differently should a similar event arise again.

Jot down the experiences you faced. What good or positive action can you take away from each encounter? It is best to check back in later if you are still feeling like you cannot be objective about the situation or see an action (external or internal) that you can take. If you are struggling here, refer back to the emotional diagnostic tool under Creating Habit Awareness to help you reframe your thoughts.

3. What can I change (that is within my power) to improve?

Many of us live in this vast illusion that we can control much more in life than is possible. You can control your choices, mindset, and actions—that's about it. Much of life is largely out of your control.

Regardless, we love to put expectations on situations that dictate our well-being. A great example is: "I will be happy when I get a raise." Even better: "I just will not be satisfied until I get ____." **You may not even realize it, but as soon as you allow an external situation (or other people) to drive your behavior, you give your power away.**

Consider the circumstances from the day or the week. What can you change that is within your control? What small, yet significant, actions can you take to shift how you affect or respond to your environment? What can you do to *own* your impact and influence, and stop giving your power away to other people or situations?

The Power Of Reflection

When you take time to reflect, you are allowing your mind to cognitively reframe your experiences. You are also able to evaluate experiences in a more positive and productive light. The practice of reflection ideally includes a mindset that is less emotionally *attached*. You are not attached to the outcomes of the situation, only to the analysis of your experiences.

I do not recommend using reflection as a tool to flog yourself over mistakes. If you are prone to doing this, I will give you a mindset mantra to repeat (and stick to!) before, during, and after your reflection time.

Repeat to yourself: "My actions and outcomes do not define me as a person."

Everyone makes mistakes. This does not mean you are a bad person. You, like all of us, do the best you can with the information you have. You cannot change the past. You are probably not clairvoyant. Let go of that which does not serve you and focus on what you *can* control or change.

Another benefit to reflection is to see the experiences for what they are and to challenge your mindset, false beliefs, and assumptions. Take my client Aaron, for instance. When we first started our coaching journey, he really thought that one of his colleagues was out to get him. This person was definitely a trigger to some of his less-than-stellar behaviors. After journaling for two weeks, Aaron shared that he realized his colleague was intimidated by him. As a result, this person reacted defensively around him. By changing how he acted around this person, they developed a better rapport in a stunningly short period of time.

Your mindset drives your thoughts, emotions, and actions. Whether you are consciously aware of it or not, your automatic program (habitual mindset) will define your daily outcomes. **It is incredibly important for your long-term fulfillment and success that you focus on creating the internal narrative you want—not the one you don't!**

Everyone I work with also wants to know: "Should I at least try to stop doing whatever it is and make a behavior shift while I'm becoming aware too?" My answer is yes and no. Yes, it's a great idea to do your best to stop bad habits. On the other hand, don't try to create new ones in the process. Reframing and rewriting old habits is challenging enough without making it more complex right from the start.

Create Your "Stop Doing" List

When you are thinking about making changes to your habitual behavior, mindset, or anything that is blocking you strategically; I have found that it is often too much to ask for you to become aware of your target issues *and* make new habits all at the same time. Becoming more aware of your bad habits is the first step. The second step is deceptively simple: *stop doing them*.

Don't try to develop a new habit; just stop the bad one. Do not replace it with anything until you have gotten used to *not* doing the bad habit. Sometimes, it's enough just to stop doing the bad habit. We don't always have to replace it with something else.

Remember, habits are ingrained ways of thinking and behaving. For many, myself included, it is enough work just to stop the behavior that is causing your roadblock. When I had my pivot point, I didn't suddenly become super likeable with everyone overnight. The first thing I did was stop being so focused, overly formal, and results-driven when I communicated.

Think of it like changing a flat tire. You cannot add the good tire on top of the old, flat tire. It just doesn't work. You have to remove the flat tire and then put a fresh, new tire on. You have to remove the old habit before you start adding new things.

When you let go of that which is no longer serving you, sometimes all you really need to do is *let go*. With my client Mary, for example, that's all she really needed to do: just stop venting in the first place. She was oversharing in an emotional state, which is usually a recipe for disaster.

What's on your "stop doing" list? As Peter Drucker has been known to say: "If you want something new, you have to stop doing something old." For many of us, we put more emphasis on our "to do" list rather than our "stop doing" list. Based on your top three areas of focus, what can you let go of that is no longer serving you?

Removing the Roadblock

Awareness comes first, then practicing the art of stopping any bad habits you've targeted. After you have mastered this, now is the time to create a new habit (if you need to) in order to see the career results you want. When I made my career transformation, I knew I had to grow my interpersonal skills. I needed to develop a mindset shift that values fellow employees as people I care about personally. I had to let go of my critical, results-driven way of communicating, and I had to show more empathy. How I "showed up" for other people had to change.

For some professionals, developing new habits is often desirable and sometimes necessary. Let's say you struggle to listen with intent. Instead, you listen for the first pause so you can add whatever you want to say. You are only listening to reply. If I were to coach you, we would work on becoming aware first. That way, you can practice stopping your habit of interrupting at the first possible moment. This is a great step, but it's not quite enough for you to significantly improve on listening with intent. Once you have mastered retraining yourself from interrupting most of the time, we can then work on what it means to listen with intent.

Growth is a process. What if I asked you to stop interrupting, become aware, and listen with intent all at once? You might be able to make some headway, but it would be a more complex task. As I have learned over many years of leading corporate cultural changes, **complexity doesn't equal sustainability**. It must be simple, specific, and straightforward for sustainability.

It should come as no surprise that developing a new habit takes practice. What might surprise you is that your body and brain will fight you to keep a "normal" state of being. It is a part of your automatic programming. Your brain likes to save energy; that's why habits exist. Imagine how stressful it would be to learn the same thing from scratch every day.

The challenge happens when we want to change. Our brains and bodies have gotten used to a certain way of being. How you think and feel creates certain chemicals in your brain and body. Your physiological state gets used to this. When you attempt to change, your body thinks there is something wrong and tries to hold on to "normal" (even if it's bad for you). This is the reason we find it hard to change when we are first trying to form new habits or stop bad ones.

It takes intentional focus and diligence to develop new patterns. This is one reason why I wrote this book. A process is achievable as long as it is repeatable. Without it, your brain and body might fight your good intentions, which could result in failure. Don't worry—I have good news! There is a formula (covered in the next chapter) to help you start and sustain successful habit shifts.

Chapter 7: Your Success Pathway

*"We are what we repeatedly do.
Excellence, then, is not an act, but a habit."*
- Will Durant

Making a Successful Shift

Now comes the fun work of creating new habits! Keep in mind that you do not have to be perfect to start developing a new habit. I encourage my clients to start this step once they have become aware, stopped the bad habit at least 70–80% of the time, and feel confident that they can develop a new one. How you *feel* about your self-improvement plan matters. Your attitude and your feelings will make or break your success. **You can dread change, or it can excite you—it is your choice to make.**

In order to make the process of shifting your mindset and behavior more fun and less like work, consider the following:

- You can view change as a gift you are giving yourself.
- Remember that self-care starts with investing in yourself.
- You cannot give what you do not have.

- Make the process a game and reward yourself for achievements.

When I experienced my own personal transformation, the process itself was enough to fuel my desire to continue on the journey of self-discovery and self-improvement. Once I realized how powerful small, yet significant, shifts in my mindset and behavior really were, I was instantly hooked. I had no idea that I had this much impact over my life and could increase my influence this way. I certainly had no idea that becoming a better version of myself could elevate me into leadership. Quite honestly, I didn't realize it could be that easy or self-rewarding!

Developing Habit Control

As you heighten your awareness and practice preempting bad behaviors, you are slowly shrinking the well-established neural pathway. While scientists say that "neurons that fire together wire together," the opposite is also true. Neurons that no longer fire together, no longer wire together. **The more times you catch yourself to stop the habit before it rears its head, intentionally shift your mindset, and practice new ways of thinking and behaving—the more you create new habits and discard the old ones.**

Habit control requires constant vigilance. For the first few weeks, it takes more energy. That is normal because you are developing new habits. Do not expect to achieve perfection overnight. You will slip up from time to time and that's fine. The more often that you catch yourself and redirect your mindset, make a different choice, or stop the behavior; you are making progress.

New habits take practice! I remember the first time I went to a cardio kickboxing class. Half the time, I felt like I was flailing around like a woman drowning in thin air. The next time, it wasn't quite as bad. As weeks went by, I went from horrible to pretty darn good. Letting go of bad habits and creating new ones is the same way: it takes practice.

Here's what doesn't work:

- Trying for a week and then giving up because you didn't attain 100% perfection.
- Using every slip into old habits as an excuse to prove to yourself that you can't do it.
- Using the awareness phase to tell yourself how terrible you are and make yourself feel bad.

Your mindset is the biggest contributing factor to your success. Like Henry Ford said: "Whether you think you can or whether you think you can't, you're probably right." We rarely outperform our own self-expectations. If you are struggling with habit control, consider how long you have had it. The longer you have had your bad habit, the harder it probably is to shift and relearn new ways of thinking, communicating, and behaving.

During the habit control phase, enlisting support from your allies becomes even more important. If you have a mentor, this is something that they can definitely help you with. Mentors are typically people we respect, so you are more likely to listen to this person's words of wisdom than anyone else. Friends and colleagues can help encourage you while holding you accountable. Coaching is also effective for getting fast transformational results.

The Secret To Successful Behavioral Habit Shifts

Let's dive into more detail about how to develop habit control at the physiological and neurological levels to increase your chances of success. You have already figured out that habits aren't changed overnight. You know that it takes awareness and practice to develop new neural pathways. What we haven't discussed yet is the shocking fact that your body will fight to keep the habit you are trying to kick and how to win!

Every emotion is a chemical mixture that gets pumped into your body. Your body does not judge whether this mixture is good or bad. When you change your mindset (and hence your emotional "mixture"), all your body knows is that there is a difference and it will attempt to keep what it has defined as "normal". In order to combat this, you need to have an intentional plan of action.

Let's say you have a goal of becoming a better listener. What's missing is the "how." Therefore, it is important to understand the *process* by which to become a better listener.

There are two main types of goals: outcome and process-oriented. Most people simply focus on the outcome ("I want to be a better listener") and that's it. Few actually break that down into the process required to achieve the outcome. Let's examine the framework you will need to establish and achieve your goal.

Step 1: Set Specific Goals. No matter what you are trying to accomplish, being specific is important. If your outcome goal is "become a better listener," perhaps a more specific goal might be: "listen with intent." I recommend that you also include a timeframe to achieve your goal. A great example might be: "I want to listen with intent in 85% of all conversations within 30 days."

Step 2: Establish the Process. Let's take the example of listening with intent. Can you identify what behaviors indicate that you are listening with intent and what actions you need to take? Break down your new habit into incremental pieces. For increased accuracy, create a checklist to include all of the processes involved in listening with intent. For instance:

- Focus on the person speaking.
- Exhibit body language that indicates you are listening (nodding head, leaning forward, etc.).
- Do not interrupt the person speaking.
- Try to silence the "inner narrative" while others speak.
- Do not constantly think only about what you are going to say next.
- Ask clarifying questions to help you understand.

Step 3: Establish a Feedback Mechanism. It is almost impossible to sustain your energies towards a goal if you have no idea *how* you are doing. In order to maintain your focus and understand your gains, you must track your progress. Daily journaling is a great method to do this. You can note how well you are performing against the targets you have set to achieve your goal. Alternatively, you can track your process on a spreadsheet to be more specific about how you performed in certain areas.

In the listening with intent example, you can see if you perform well in all the other areas each day, but struggle to stay focused on what the person is saying. This gives you useful information that helps fine-tune your internal work.

Step 4: Enlist Allies for Support. It is helpful to connect with people who are like-minded and maybe even have the same goals as you do. This is one of the reasons for the existence of running clubs, cycling clubs, book clubs, and almost any group activity. It not only encourages you to stay on track, but also motivates you by seeing how well other people are progressing in their work. In addition, when you have setbacks or challenges, you will have someone to talk to about it and help you overcome your hurdle.

You also want to identify those who might sabotage your efforts. These are people who might have something to lose because of your new habit. Saboteurs are not always obvious. Let's say you have a habit of complaining about coworkers with a close colleague. That colleague enjoys complaining and talking about other people. This person will probably encourage the bad habit you want to stop.

Step 5: Create Implementation Intentions. You can make developing your new habit almost effortless by creating implementation intentions. These are specific trigger-based instructions that you write down to confirm when, where, and how you will act on your new habit. In order to become someone that listens with intent in our earlier example, you might write down: "When someone speaks to me, I will focus on them, not interrupt, and clarify or add my thoughts only when I know that they have finished speaking."

Research has shown that by writing your intentions, you are much more likely to achieve the goal.[11] This process is also useful if you experience an interruption and need to restart your personal growth work. You can create an implementation intention that specifically outlines what you will do if you are interrupted in developing your new habit.

The Secret to Success Is Support

You can certainly achieve a lot of great things on your own. You will also progress much further and faster by getting help from others. When you start your elevation journey of change, share your goals with those you trust and who are willing to support you. You will be surprised at how many people in your community want to aid your growth!

If it surprises you that people want to help you get better, consider this: by trying to be a better version of yourself, you

---

[11] Dr. Gail Matthews, "Goals Research Summary," Dominican University of California, *https://www.dominican.edu/sites/default/files/2020-02/gailmatthews-harvard-goals-researchsummary.pdf.*

are also being less of whatever it is that annoys those around you. Of course they will want to help you out! Remember my client, Mary? She enlisted the support of her entire department in a complaint-free challenge to not only help her stop venting, but also to provide a collaborative platform for others to achieve the same goal.

By starting this community challenge, Mary was doing three very important things at once. One, she was getting support for her goal of removing complaining from her behavior. Two, she made her goal public so other people would notice the change in her behavior. You definitely don't want to expend energy in making a shift only to have people still expect the same behavior from you! Three, Mary sent a clear message as a leader to her teams that complaining is not appreciated and that she was leading the change by modeling the behavior.

This final point is important, particularly if you are a leader. Whatever behavior you demonstrate sets the standard for those reporting to you. Mary noticed that her team also whined quite a bit. They seemed to have no problem with complaining about other people in the organization (or anything else). Ironically, this became more obvious to Mary when she started developing awareness about her *own* habitual behaviors.

You can try something similar or just share your goal with trusted colleagues. For example, ask them to tell you when you slip up or even aid you in developing awareness. Your behavioral and/or mindset shift will be much more efficient with help! After all, our blind spots are difficult for us to see; this is not so for other people.

If you make the process a game between you and your allies, that's when the change becomes more fun! In Mary's case, she had an entire department working together to try and become complaint-free in order to win prizes for how well they did. Whenever you can get support to become a better version of yourself, it is a lot easier and much more sustainable.

If you do not share your goals, it is easier to backslide or completely give up. After all, no one will notice because you haven't actually changed anything! However, if you involve an accountability buddy or two, then it is harder to simply let go of your goal. **A goal shared is a goal achieved.** It is our basic human nature to thrive from support and avoid disappointing others.

Celebrate Your Wins

Behavior and mindset shifts are boring unless you acknowledge and celebrate them. Not only does the process automatically become more positive, it's also more noticeable. You are with yourself all the time. You may not notice the change in you without setting specific milestones along your journey to becoming better.

This is true for many different aspects of personal change. If you are trying to lose weight, for example, the change is slow, and you may not notice it. However, when you meet a friend who hasn't seen you in weeks, they might exclaim how much thinner you look!

Set mini milestones for yourself. Leverage your daily journal to understand how often you exhibit the problem behavior or mindset and how well you are performing against your goal. Let's say during your awareness phase, for instance, you caught yourself interrupting someone five times a day on average. You can set a mini milestone to celebrate when you see a 50% decrease in the target behavior.

How you celebrate is up to you. It is most important that you acknowledge your accomplishments. Treat yourself to something that gives you joy or energy. If you have enlisted the aid of your allies to achieve your behavior shift, celebrate with them too! After all, they have probably been the ones giving you feedback on your improvements. Tackling problem habits is tough and it is much more fun with friends.

One day, I said to my best friend, "I'm terrible at asking for help." My friend looked back at me with a wry twinkle in her eye and she said, "No kidding!" Starting that day, she helped me with being okay with asking for and accepting help. What is even more heartwarming is that she was really happy to work with me on making a successful behavioral and mindset shift.

Whenever I forget and go on autopilot, my friend reminds me: "You don't always have to be strong, Erin. It's okay to accept help." That means a lot to me. Whatever you are working on in your career or your life, remember that you can lean on your support network. People are more willing to help than you think!

Sustain Your Gains

"How long before I will see success with my behavior shift, Coach?" my client David asked. David, like many of us, wanted a timeline to achieve his goals. While developing a new habit varies from person to person, research indicates that the average timeline is around 66 days.[12] **You will know you have developed a habit when your new behavior becomes automatic.** You have achieved success when you really don't have to think about your new behavior; it feels natural.

Interestingly, it is also incredibly easy to slip back into old habits. In order to stop yourself from self-sabotaging, stick to your journaling or logging. For all my clients, journaling is a daily routine that helps them stay on track. Please do not rely solely on those around you to tell you that you've strayed from your target.

Why is it so easy to fall back into old habits? Quite simply, your brain has built that particular strong neural pathway and it takes time before it is "pruned." This is a process of removing

---

[12] Phillippa Lally, Cornelia H. M. van Jaarsveld, Henry W. W. Potts, and Jane Wardle, "How are habits formed: Modelling habit formation in the real world," *European Journal of Social Psychology* 40, no. 10 (October 2010): https://doi.org/10.1002/ejsp.674, https://onlinelibrary.wiley.com/doi/abs/10.1002/ejsp.674.

synaptic connections between neurons that are no longer needed.

Historically, scientists thought that this was a process that ends with adolescents; research has discovered that pruning also occurs in adults, but not as aggressively.[13]

In order to stick to the narrative that you want, journaling (or logging) is a lifesaver. It helps you stay on track and be intentional about your daily actions. I journal every day if at all possible. I'm also kind to myself and realize that life happens. As I remind my clients, skipping one day does not mean that you are a failure. Set your implementation intention and revisit your journal the next day.

Have a structure to your journaling/logging process. Make this happen with intent! To refresh, here's what I recommend including in your journal:

- Start with gratitude to establish the right internal atmosphere.
- Note your triggers or emotional reactions and acknowledge the emotion without judgement.
- Reframe any unwanted or destructive thought patterns, while removing distortions.

---

[13] Professor Rusty Gage, "Adult brain prunes branched connections of new neurons," Salk Institute, May 2, 2016, *https://www.salk.edu/news-release/adult-brain-prunes-branched-connections-of-new-neurons/*.

- Note how you performed against your target habit shift.
- Don't beat yourself up for not being perfect.
- Objectively observe any opportunities to improve and note actions that you can take to realize your goal.

What you decide to include in your journal beyond this list is entirely up to you. Some clients wrap up with additional gratitude or any revelations they had after completing an entry. Others take this time to reflect on the entire day and process what they learned. Some find it useful to also leverage this tool to help them prioritize the next day's tasks. It is *your* journal. Make it your own and include what is meaningful to you.

Another powerful outcome of journaling is that you have a written chronicle of your improvement. Therefore, I recommend looking back in your journal as you progress to see the change in your written dialogue. Because we improve incrementally, this will not be drastically noticeable overnight or from day to day. However, as the days compound, you will see changes in what you say in your journal and the results you report.

If you get stuck, it's important to lean on your support group. For my clients that have difficulty letting go, we examine the potential root cause. Occasionally, additional work is needed to identify the reason we respond in certain ways. You may have what feels like a compulsion to act or an extreme aversion. Connect with a certified and licensed resource to help you work through something that you feel might be buried too deep to tackle on your own.

What's Next?

For almost every client I work with, the question is often, "What's next?" Realizing your own ability to elevate your career is empowering and uplifting! There's no real reason to stop being a better human being. **There's no reason to stop elevating your career.** You do not have to tackle mountains of change at once (it's better for everyone if you don't). You can make big impacts with small shifts. Maybe "what's next" for you is the next item from your feedback list or something you've always wanted to do differently.

Whatever it is, remember that change isn't like a rocket ship taking off; it's more like climbing stairs. You will learn a little, apply it, adjust it, absorb it, and then master it before you see more results. It's common to feel like you've hit a plateau and then suddenly have a breakthrough moment. It's also a great idea to learn from failure. Not everything will work wonderfully the first time and that's not a bad thing. We learn best by applying and adjusting based on the feedback from our environment.

Refresh your mind occasionally with the processes and notes from this book to help you along your way. Don't forget the resources online at my website coacheurban.com or elevateyourcareerbook.com. I'm very excited about your journey to elevate your career for more impact and income — here's to "what's next" for you!

Chapter 8: Fast-Track Your Growth

*"Only those who will risk going too far can possibly find out
how far one can go."*
- T. S. Eliot

Get Real Results Right Away

In our instant gratification society, we expect immediate results. I have great news: you *can* get immediate results with a successful behavioral shift! I know that if I had received the pivotal feedback that changed my entire career (and my life) from a person I *respected*, I would have seen much faster results. In addition, if my feedback debriefing came from a person qualified to better manage its psychological stages, I could have accelerated my growth within 30 days or less.

To prove this point, I have done exactly that with my clients. All of my clients notice immediate results after applying seemingly simple shifts in their behavior. You can unlock your potential to achieve more influence and impact quite quickly. Ask yourself: are you willing to follow the process that delivers results and dedicate yourself to change? If this sounds like a challenge you are up for, this chapter identifies exactly how to get rapid results.

Stage 1: Feedback

First, you need to receive feedback on your behavior. Without it, you are taking a shot in the dark and you may or may not get real results right away. If you take a wild guess at something, you will get results, but they may not be the ones you wanted or make that much of an impression on your career.

It's best to rip the blindfold off and have data to define your behavioral targets. The most efficient way to do this is by getting insights into your perceived behavior from those you work with as referenced in Chapter 5: Identify Your Roadblocks.

Stage 2: Identify the Gap

During your feedback debriefing, identify the biggest gap. If you have two areas of equal rating, pick the one that is most strategically important to your career growth. Choose only *one* habit to work on because you want to be as laser-focused on that change as possible. Tackling more than one area is more complex and, therefore, takes longer. **In order to see real, quick results, stick to one area to improve.**

Be sure to reexamine the guides I provided in Chapters 5 and 6 on how to best go about obtaining your feedback and debriefing the information. I highly recommend getting qualified assistance in this process to ensure optimal results.

Stage 3: Enlist Your Allies

To achieve the quickest positive outcomes, I recommend enlisting your supporters immediately. The faster you engage other people in changing your habits and removing your roadblocks to growth, the faster you will see results. This also makes the next step go a lot quicker because you will receive valuable real-time feedback during the awareness phase.

Do you have work colleagues that can give you valuable tips along the way on how you are performing with your goals? What about your boss or a mentor? Ideally your partner in success is someone (or several people) who work with you on a weekly basis. While they do not have to see you every day, it is best if they are a part of your work stream.

Stage 4: Awareness for Baseline

Establish your baseline and understand the behavior you want to change. The exact steps we identified in Chapter 6 to create awareness and log your triggers apply here as well. You want to develop a daily log, note your trigger, and identify the emotion associated with it along with your raw immediate thoughts.

If you desire change, it's more productive to be aware *ahead* of time with the behavior you are working on rather than realizing it in hindsight. Your allies can help you with insights and details to deepen your understanding and further your results.

Stage 5: Your "Stop Doing" List

With almost every behavioral shift, there is something you can stop doing. What is the habit that you need to let go of? In our earlier example, my client Mary just needed to stop venting to her team. There are a lot of results you can gain from just halting a bad behavior!

Sometimes, behavior shifts are very simple on the surface. You might think, for example, that you need to complain less, listen better, or smile more. Superficially, some habits are pretty obvious; these are easier to contain and, therefore, eliminate. It's still worth knowing what triggers those habits so you do not experience a relapse under stress.

Stage 6: Behavioral Shift and New Habits

In most cases, it's also important to develop better habits to replace the bad ones. Ending bad habits is great. However, that's rarely all you need to do. Let's just say you succeed in stopping yourself from obnoxiously interrupting people. It's also very likely that you struggle to listen with intent. This is a new behavior you can work on to improve.

Any new habit can be developed over time with repeated practice. The more you work at it, the easier it becomes, and the less you have to actually think about it.

Stage 7: Sustain Your Gains

How fast people can develop a new habit varies from person to person. If you continue your daily/weekly log and enlist support, you have an infinitely better chance of success. More importantly, you will also see faster results. It's not uncommon to see significant results in 30 days (or less) for those who are truly motivated to change, and sustained change within 60 days or less.

How will you know that you have achieved success? The new behavior is successful when it becomes automatic. Reference the "Sustain Your Gains" section in Chapter 7 for more insight.

Such habits, whether they be internal (mindset) or external actions, are simply programmed ways of thinking and behaving. From the minute you challenge your programming, you are starting to fire and wire new neurons! While forming a new habit takes time and intentional focus, you will be amazed at how much change you can actually make.

Your Internal Atmosphere

While this isn't a stage per se, it's still essential for your growth. You can think of it as the soil that fertilizes your change or the foundation on which you build upon. Your internal atmosphere must include a growth mindset. I'm not going to pound you with a host of empty platitudes about how you have to be positive or repeat mantras. What I *will* say is that when you don't believe you can do something, it is not likely you will outperform your expectations.

If you have a problem with self-confidence, self-worth, or self-care, it will impact your results. You can start to produce massive positive change by challenging the negative self-labels you've created. If you have automatic negative thoughts (ANTs), turn them into positive empowering thoughts (PETs). There's a catchphrase common in the world of brain-based positive psychology: "Turn your ANTs into PETs." (I can't say that without chuckling a little.)

How you challenge your negative beliefs is almost identical to how you can better capture and manage your raw thoughts with the diagnostic tool I provided in Chapter 6 under "Getting Started on Your Shift". You want to record your negative thought exactly as it is being expressed in your mind. Then, look for distortions. Is it factual? What biases do you see? Finally, rewrite it in a positive way that is empowering to you.

This short, simple process is called cognitive reframing (or restructuring) and it's extremely effective. If you struggle with reframing your negative thoughts, think about how your best friend might write it for you. We are rarely our own best friends.

Leverage your logical brain to challenge negative labels by journaling or logging your negative thought patterns and reframing them. If this practice is repeated on a daily or weekly basis, you will start to see shifts in your mindset. The more often you challenge your automatic negative thoughts (ANTs) and turn them into positive empowering thoughts (PETs), the faster you will see results.

Remember, all habits (mental and physical) are neural pathways that have strengthened through repetition. Therefore, repetition can create new ones too!

Communicating Your Intent Is Critical

In order to see real results right away, it is critical to communicate your intent with as many people as possible. The people who you work with have identified and categorized your persona. In their minds, they *believe* you will act in a certain way. The challenge is that even if you make a dramatic change, they may not notice. People tend to filter out what is counter to their own belief structure, hence the saying, "You get what you expect."

When people expect certain responses, their brain filters inputs accordingly. For example, if you have decided that someone is out to get you, no matter what they do, your brain will be looking for proof that they mean you harm. That's the way our brains work. As Jennice Vilhauer, PhD, writes in *Psychology Today*: "One of the reasons our expectations keep us so stuck is that we have the automatic tendency to use the past to predict the future."[14]

---

[14] Jennice Vilhauer, "How to Get What You Really Want: Changing your outlook and overcoming self-fulfilling prophecies," *Psychology Today*,

Other people have developed a perception of you based on your past behaviors. This drives your credibility. You will need to communicate your intent to change a behavior and to encourage them to look for a difference. However, be aware of your situation and whom is involved. As one of my clients, Dora, found out—sometimes we need to be discrete.

Dora has the exact opposite work style of her boss, and it made their interactions very tense. While my client preferred to think on things, do research, and come up with an exact answer, her boss was impatient, action-oriented, demanding, and very critical.

Dora said that she felt sick to her stomach whenever she had to meet with her boss. I gave her a few key changes in how she approached what she said to him. Immediately after their next meeting, she called me to exclaim that she was shocked by how well it went. "He responded so much better, and he was actually nice to me!" she said.

Obviously, Dora did not want to announce that she was changing her communication approach with him because of their already tense relationship. Regardless, the outcome was strikingly different and immediately noticeable. On the other hand, if you've developed a reputation for a certain type of behavior, it doesn't hurt to raise other people's awareness of a change.

December 18, 2015, *https://www.psychologytoday.com/us/blog/living-forward/201512/how-get-what-you-really-want.*

Take Strategically Calculated Risks

While I was seeing results after my major career wake-up call, I knew I needed to increase the level of awareness that I was different and looking to grow my career. It was important that I challenge the status quo and make *other people* fire and wire new neurons! I intentionally took a strategic risk and applied for a senior-level role that I knew I wouldn't get.

The reason was very simple. The management team knew me for what I had done for the company. They judged my future potential on my past performance. They also had no idea what I was capable of because I didn't use all of my abilities in my role at the time. Unless I made it obvious, no one would know that I *wanted* to elevate my career. Basically, I had to create a catalyst to ignite change. Otherwise, I would be a victim of habitual thinking: mine and my management's.

As a matter of protocol, I received interviews with key decision-makers. Because this was an SVP position, one of those interviews was with the CEO. He asked me very politely why I applied for the role. I told him the truth: "I know this position is a stretch and that is not why I applied. I also know that you have no idea what I'm capable of unless we have a conversation about it. You know me for what I do on a daily basis and that is only a fraction of what I can accomplish for this company."

The CEO looked thoughtful and he said: "You are extremely smart for having the courage to apply for a role you know is a stretch. I'm proud of you. What do you want to do?" This opened the door for us to have a very productive discussion on what I was passionate about and how I could help the organization. Less than six months later, they created a leadership position that was strategically important for the entire company and promoted me to the role.

I cannot stress enough how essential it is to communicate your intent, particularly if you want to elevate your career. If you remain silent and hope other people will notice, you are assuming that they don't think that you are perfectly happy right where you are. Do not expect other people to read your mind: communicate your goals!

The Elevator Pitch Isn't Dead

The last tool I want to arm you with is the art of the elevator pitch. When you start making positive changes in yourself, prepare to have succinct and impactful conversations when it matters. While I'd like to say that successful people are where they are due to some exciting combination of talents, most of them are successful *in spite of themselves*. **Often, great careers are built on chance encounters or calculated risks. It always pays to be prepared.**

There are three parts to an elevator pitch:

1. **Opener:** Your name, your role, and what you do (condensed; no one wants to listen to a biography).
2. **Intent:** This is followed by what you want to do and/or how you want to add value to the company.
3. **Your why:** End by explaining why you are a great fit for that type of work (skills, expertise, etc.).

The opener is fairly self-explanatory. However, an outstanding elevator pitch includes a highly concise and specific description of what you intend to achieve. This can be either in your current role or in a future position. I leveraged part of this in the interview with the CEO for the role I knew I wouldn't get. You must be *specific* if you want a certain type of position. If you decide to have a more generalized statement such as "I want to lead a team", then you better have a great follow-up with your why.

An example of a succinct and specific elevator pitch with intent is: "I want to lead a team to innovate how we do business with international accounts." I do not always encourage professionals to be too title-focused, such as: "I want to be the SVP of Operations." Say this to the wrong person and it can hurt more than help you. No one wants to feel like their job is threatened by your ambitions!

One of my clients performed this very blunder before she connected with me for coaching. "I was in the interview and I was asked where I saw myself in 3–5 years, so I told them, Chief Production Lead," she said. The problem was that the Chief Production Lead was in the interview. She didn't get that job. She also never repeated that mistake again!

You must articulate your career growth intent as often as possible (and when appropriate), but conserve your full elevator pitch for the ideal moment. You can discuss your intent in a casual conversation or in more formal settings, like a professional development mentoring meeting. It's always more effective when you are truly excited or passionate about something. This will catch on, and your allies will be more apt to help you.

In addition, when you express what you want to do with your career, it plants seeds in the minds of your allies, management, and network. For example, if you say that you are passionate about improving how the company does business (and maybe you participate in a few process-improvement projects), that generates momentum in other people's minds. They have an idea of what to look for to help you grow. It helps your network send you to the right connections. It gives your managers an idea of the roles you are a good fit to grow into.

Keep your *full* elevator pitch reserved for those chance encounters with key decision-makers. For example, if you have a few moments with an executive you rarely meet, be prepared to deliver it. Ideally, you will have practiced this, so it is second nature. Fumble it and your credibility is toast. Be concise and do not fluff, explain, or backpedal! The entire elevator pitch should not exceed three sentences.

For example: "It's nice you meet you. My name is Dari Young, and I'm the Senior Analyst for XWZ account. My goal is to lead a European investments team for our international business unit. I have proven experience in the European market and successfully led several special project teams."

You will notice the absolute absence of any bragging in this statement. Everything stated is factual. At no time was there any mention of how awesome the person is. With that being said, it is perfectly acceptable to mention your performance from a factual point of view. If you consistently exceed expectations in a certain expertise, then say so. If you are requested to provide more information, be prepared to do so. You might be asked about your contributions. Have two or three of your top wins ready to go at a moment's notice with explicit impacts to the business.

There are multiple benefits to having a concise and specific elevator pitch. For one, it helps you focus your career goals. Another is increasing your confidence and preparing you for opportunities should they arise.

More Impact, More Income

As you shift your behaviors to reflect your desires, you will also increase your influence. Bettering your behavioral impact always includes deepening your credibility with others. I have never heard anyone say: "Gee, Bobbi is much better to work with; that's awful." Increased credibility with others is a natural by-product of being a better you!

If you aren't sure about this, let's put it this way: how likely are you to like and trust someone who has a really annoying behavior issue? Or, how likely is it that you are easily influenced by someone you do *not* like or trust? You might do what they want because you have to, but you will probably only do the bare minimum to get by (and so you don't have to deal with them anymore).

Let's take this a step further. When you become more likeable, you will also positively influence others more as a result. Everyone impacts other people. Unfortunately, most of it is unintentional because we aren't *thinking* about it. As a result, our impact is either irresponsible, happenstance, counter to what we want, or (at worst) toxic. This is a terrible waste.

Basically, if you do not manage perceptions – it will manage *you*.

What if you can become more intentional about your impact? I'm glad that you think that's important because that's *exactly* what happens when you start becoming more self-aware about your behaviors! See what I did there? Yes, you are becoming more intentional just by following the process of becoming a better version of you. It follows naturally that you now have more *intentional* impact. This means that your impact is more often the result you want versus the result you don't.

By now, you are probably wondering about the "More Income" part of this section. That flows as a natural result of working on your behaviors as well. How likely is it that you will be elevated into a leadership role if you have gaps in your persona? While historically there have been many unfortunate promotions of toxic bosses, thankfully, that time is fading.

Companies are paying closer attention to their workplace environments. When you are interviewed for a new job, for example, much more attention is being paid to who you *are* versus what you have done. As our workplace cultures evolve, the chances of professionals with interpersonal issues being elevated into leadership roles will become less common.

Besides, if you have a gap in your credibility, it's unlikely that people will follow you as a leader. You may be a boss, but you will never *lead*. Leadership requires a high degree of trust, credibility, and interpersonal abilities. Leadership is not about being a technical expert, working hard, being the best, or telling other people what to do. Effective leadership is primarily about being a *people* expert.

As you work on yourself and leverage the tools that I have provided, you will also start to become better leadership material. This is simply because you are working on your interpersonal skills. You are fine-tuning your ability to manage perceptions. You are becoming better with other people. Regardless, if you have no desire to move into a formal leadership role, that's perfectly fine.

The great news is that whether or not you want to move into a leadership role doesn't mean that your income won't increase. More income simply means that, as a natural outgrowth of your ability to intentionally impact others, you are more likely to attract positive attention. Other people tend to gravitate to those that are more intentional with their impact and are easier to work with. Elevating your career doesn't *just* mean moving into leadership roles.

My client, Anna, needed a salary raise to match the level of work she was doing. Before she met me, she had received feedback that she was too direct in her delivery and that she needed to soften her message with people. She had burned a few bridges already. As a project manager, she was known for "getting things done." This unfortunately reinforced her naturally blunt and direct approach for too many years. Finally, she realized that she was feeling stuck in her career and her coworkers were avoiding her.

After a few weeks of working with me, one of her more open coworkers asked Anna: "What happened to you? You are a different person to be around!" By focusing on a few important behavior shifts, Anna made a big difference with her team and her boss. When performance review time came, she also got the raise that she had been wanting. Now, her salary is commensurate with the work that she is performing. As a plus, her work collaboration is much smoother and, therefore, "getting things done" is a lot easier to do.

You don't have to move mountains to make a massive difference in your professional career and your life. Go on, turn off your autopilot program to see just how far you can elevate your career for more impact and more income!

Works Cited

Antoun, Michael, et al. "The acute physiological stress response to driving: A systematic review," *PLoS One* 12, no. 10 (2017): e0185517, *https://www.ncbi.nlm.nih.gov/pmc/articles/PMC5642886/*

Gage, Rusty. "Adult brain prunes branched connections of new neurons," Salk Institute, May 2, 2016, *https://www.salk.edu/news-release/adult-brain-prunes-branched-connections-of-new-neurons/*.

Gardner, Howard "Cracking Open the IQ Box." *The American Prospect*, (Winter 1995).

Goldsmith, Marshall *What Got You Here Won't Get You There* (Hachette Books, 2014), 8.

Goleman, Daniel *Emotional Intelligence* (Bantam Books, 2006), 36.

Klaus, Peggy. *The Hard Truth About Soft Skills: Workplace Lessons Smart People Wish They'd Learned Sooner.* HarperCollins, 2007.

Lally, Phillippa, et al. "How are habits formed: Modelling habit formation in the real world," *European Journal of Social Psychology* 40, no. 10 (October 2010): *https://doi.org/10.1002/ejsp.674*, *https://onlinelibrary.wiley.com/doi/abs/10.1002/ejsp.674*.

Matthews, Gail. "Goals Research Summary," Dominican University of California, *https://www.dominican.edu/sites/default/files/2020-02/gailmatthews-harvard-goals-researchsummary.pdf.*

Morris, Shila "Are You Really a Team Leader?" The John Maxwell Team, *https://johnmaxwellteam.com/are-you-really-a-team-leader/.*

Pennington, Rob. *https://drrobpennington.com/.* LinkedIn: *https://www.linkedin.com/in/robertpenningtonphd/.*

Vilhauer, Jennice. "How to Get What You Really Want: Changing your outlook and overcoming self-fulfilling prophecies," *Psychology Today*, December 18, 2015, *https://www.psychologytoday.com/us/blog/living-forward/201512/how-get-what-you-really-want.*

"Cognitive restructuring," Wikipedia, *https://en.wikipedia.org/wiki/Cognitive_restructuring.*

"Kübler-Ross model," Wikipedia, *https://en.wikipedia.org/wiki/K%C3%BCbler-Ross_model.*